Anonymous

Shakespeare

A Revelation

Anonymous

Shakespeare
A Revelation

ISBN/EAN: 9783337063337

Printed in Europe, USA, Canada, Australia, Japan

Cover: Foto ©ninafisch / pixelio.de

More available books at **www.hansebooks.com**

SHAKESPEARE

A REVELATION

BY

?

LONDON
SKEFFINGTON & SON, PICCADILLY
Publishers to H.M. The Queen and to H.R.H. The Prince of Wales
1897

SHAKESPEARE

CHAPTER I

THE meeting that evening of the Chicago Historical Society was a great success. The ever interesting—nay, exciting—subject of the authorship of Shakespeare's Plays and Poems had been discussed after the reading of a paper by Mr Geoffrey Courthope. The great Donnelly himself, the ingenious author of *The Great Cryptogram*, had made out a strong case, founded on premises, the truth of which, if admitted, rendered it unassailable; but he had been answered in due course by an anti-Baconian. When the motion was put from the chair, twenty-one voted for it and nineteen against, and the fair fame of William Shakespeare would have received the endorsement of the Chicago Historical Society, when the Major arose in his place and explained his desire to put on record that, when he gave his vote, he was under the impression it was with the Noes and not, as it had since been explained to him, with the Ayes; and the question, so far as Chicago and the rest of the world are concerned, still remained unsettled.

When the meeting broke up, Geoffrey Courthope and a couple of his friends left together, and, at the invitation of the former, finished the evening at his pleasant bachelor mansion in Michigan Avenue. Courthope was unmarried and very rich. He was, moreover, twenty-five years of age and all alone in the world; for his devoted parents had left him the legacies of a sweet nature, a studious mind and many millions of dollars. He still retained the first, and his mind he had further stored by learning; but his fortune might have been seriously affected if it had not been so large, for he had a hobby, and hobbies are expensive. His was Shakespeare; and Geoffrey's mind was fully receptive to the beautiful, and keenly sensitive to the philosophy and humanity of the Poet and Playwright.

During his Harvard College course he had

fallen in love with him to the adoration point, and in his more matured years he had studied and analysed him as few students of Shakespeare had done. One form of his passion took shape in the desire to possess early editions and literary memorials of the Poet and his contemporaries, and a goodly library was the result. If a relic of the poet could be obtained, no sum was too large for Geoffrey to give for it—and such relics, remotely or nearly associated with the beloved object, accumulated in Geoffrey's possession, until a museum of more or less veracious memorials had been formed. He had made two pilgrimages to Stratford, and would have brought back to Chicago the house in which Shakespeare was born, and the Hathaway cottage at Shottery, if his money could have bought them.

He was indeed an enthusiast, and would have remained true to his idol but that the critical faculty in him raised doubts in his mind regarding the true authorship of the Poems and Plays. He directed his mind to analysis. He read all the works of all the authors, critics, commentators and cavillers on the subject. New renderings of obscure passages and words were familiar to him. He sought for meanings apart from manifest and plain renderings. He had many theories and was unsatisfied.

Let us go back to the three friends at Geoffrey's house.

'The Shakespeare mystery remains as impenetrable as ever,' said Harber.

'Why imagine a mystery at all?' was the reply. 'Surely it is enough that his works come to us with his name attached as the author, and why dispute the statement? There is no mystery whatever, my dear fellow. Depend on it, Shakespeare wrote them, and there's an end of it.'

'Apart from what Donnelly told us to-night,' said the third, 'I am firmly convinced that no other than Francis Bacon could have been the author. It is simply by the exhaustive process that I have arrived at this; for no other author or writer of the Elizabethan age was capable of it.'

'And yet,' said Geoffrey, 'in comparing the well-known works of Bacon with those so-called of Shakespeare, no resemblance is found; in fact, the style of Bacon is indicative of the man solid, judicial and penetrating, without fancy or wit, and certainly free from the playfulness of the other author, whoever he may have been. Bacon is a philosopher of another stamp, and the difference between him and the other as demonstrated in their works is so great—so divergent—as to incline one to think that Bacon never wrote a line of true poetry in his life.'

'We heard to-night,' his friend replied, 'ample argument to convince us that the man Shakespeare personated the true author. In these days of progress we want something more than tradition as an aid to truth; and in the meagre remains of the Burgess of Stratford, who was silent for fourteen years, there is nothing whatever to indicate him as the Poet of the Human Race, and as the greatest literary character the world has ever known.'

And so, with argument of a like kind, they discussed the matter far into the night; and when Geoffrey slept, after the departure of his friends, he dreamed of searching for the truth amid obstacles which baffled and difficulties which retarded—a knight-errantry on a literary field of battle—a quest for the Holy Grail, of a kind suitable to the needs of the nineteenth century and found it not. Curiously intermingled with the thread of his dream was always a fair face, which smilingly seemed to encourage him in his labour and to beam on him with those looks of love, seen by him in his daily life, perhaps, but to which before this he had never responded.

Geoffrey rose the next morning to the routine of work he had, with singular method, defined for himself. In his library, surrounded by his books, he wrote for several hours, always on the same subject—his beloved Shakespeare—debating on old theories, starting new ones, following elusive hypotheses and conjectures to find himself lost in mazes and intricacies which landed him where he had started from. But frequently his dream occurred to him, and the face of the sweet girl therein. What did it mean? Was it of the peerless Miranda, the lively Silvia, the youthful Juliet, or of another of Shakespeare's heroines? He could not say. At times he thought he had seen it before; or was it in the spirit, perhaps, a reminiscence of the past, a being perchance beyond the pale of this life, or an anticipation of the future? It was puzzling, yet pleasing; and while the face would persist in recurring to his mind's eye to the point of disturbance of his mental calm, he regretted it not, for he fancied that in this experience there might be some telepathic indication of an early meeting with its owner.

In his intimate knowledge of his beloved author he had given such attributes to his heroines as their sweet and euphonious names had suggested to him; and those who have pondered over those names will understand the full and perfect meanings conveyed by such musical words as Portia the stately, Jessica the yielding, Beatrice the sparkling and quick-witted, the aristocratic Olivia, the love-laden Viola; and who is not in love with Rosalind, not only for her beauty and charm, but also for her sweet name?

Geoffrey had sought and obtained from the brush of an artist of European reputation delineations of such beautiful women, but how far short of Geoffrey's ideals he alone knew.

And his library was a veritable storehouse of Shakesperian lore; not only all the editions of the master published in more modern times, but, with some rare and valuable folios of the seventeenth century, there were volumes yielding up the sources, perhaps, of Shakespeare's inspiration, such as the *Essays* of Montaigne, Camden's *Remains*, Painter's *Palace of Pleasure*, Holinshed's *Chronicle*, Sydney's *Arcadia*, Chaucer and Plutarch. In addition, were to be found every Life and every controversial work of modern days on the absorbing subject of the authorship itself. It was veritably a Shakespearian Library, and its studious owner was never happier than when, within the seclusion of its walls, he was far apart from the outer world of busy Chicago.

CHAPTER II

Chicago was indeed busy, for the World's Fair had just been inaugurated, and the splendid show, imperfect but yet beautiful, was advancing, with the summer season, to its maturity of form and colour. Already thousands of visitors had arrived from the Home Country and from afar. Geoffrey, as a prominent and rich citizen, had not declined to take a part in the inception and development of some of its features, and his ideas and suggestions had been adopted in those instances where his known good taste and regard for æsthetical beauty were sought to be employed. He thus was frequently called upon to visit the park in his semi-official capacity, and while fulfilling the pleasant task of assisting in the realisation of the dream of the architect, the artist and the musician, he had many opportunities of observing people, and of forming conclusions regarding them. His vivid imagination had full play among the varied types of humanity attracted to the World's Fair. He was not surprised to learn that his guesses at truth were correct among the commonplace crowd, but here and there he was startled to find the ability he possessed, or believed he possessed, to discover the unmistakably good or the unquestionably evil in man, irrespective of race or nationality.

It was a bright day in June, and the buildings and thoroughfares of the Exhibition grounds were crowded with visitors. A varying succession of sightseers of many nationalities passed in and out, to and fro, and the hum of men filled the air. Suddenly an unusual agitation seized the crowd, and the cry of Fire! was followed by a movement, undecided at first, but soon directed towards the scene of the conflagration—one of the large, beautiful, but fragile, structures which adorned the park. It had been on fire but for ten minutes—the brigade of firemen were fighting the flames, and tons of water were being pumped on to the building. There were doors of exit; and the people within had been pressing, panic-stricken, through them until the passages were blocked by the shrieking crowd. It looked like an impending great calamity, whereby hundreds would be sacrificed. At this critical time Geoffrey arrived on the scene, and discovered that, if more means of outlet were not at once made, there would indeed be a direful tragedy.

Remembering that the building was less solid than it looked, he headed a party of men who, at his instigation, and with the axes they carried, attacked its wooden sides, and soon made a breach through which poured the excited crowd of men, women and children. Geoffrey was standing on a ledge above the people shouting directions to them, while the approaching fire in the rear seemed to render their escape more unlikely. While the struggling mass was pressing forward — a veritable *sauve qui peut*—the weaker trampled on by the stronger, and men forgetting their manhood in the struggle. Geoffrey could see on the edge of the crowd a party of three —a woman and two men supporting her. A flash of reminiscence lit up his brain. The woman—who was she? And amid the lurid smoke, with a background of flame, he saw the face of the lady of his dream. Could it be possible? Nay, more, there was something like a recognition in the momentary glance as their eyes met. What could it mean? Just then Geoffrey detected a movement in the crowd which enabled him to render assistance to the girl and her friends, and in less time than it takes to tell it, they found themselves in the open air and in safety.

With a thrill of joy Geoffrey drew them away through the working firemen, the cordon of police and the outside crowd.

Naturally modest, and with the fine sense of not wishing to force his company on them, he would have retired, and yet felt reluctant to leave the side of the girl, whose face filled him with a strange and novel feeling of association and sympathy. He raised his hat, and with the commonplace remark, 'I trust you are all right now,' was about to depart, when the elder of the two men exclaimed, 'Thanks to God and to you, my daughter and I have been saved from an awful death;' and the younger one joined in with, 'And I also owe a deep debt of gratitude to one whose name I would ask, that I may know who my rescuer is.'

Whatever sense of embarrassment he had felt was thus dispelled, and Geoffrey glanced towards the girl whose soft look of gratitude and something like invitation, if one might use so strong a word, encouraged him to answer, 'I am Geoffrey Courthope, and am only too glad to have been in the park to-day to have assisted in helping you all out of a very unpleasant fix. And now, sir,' said Geoffrey, 'Let us exchange confidences, and tell me who you are.'

'My name is Layton,' the other replied, 'and this, Mr Courthope, is my daughter Doris, who, if she is silent, feels, I know, very grateful to her gallant rescuer. We are from Melbourne. This gentleman, who also owes his life to you, will, I feel sure, join us in thanking you.'

'I am grateful to you,' the other replied. 'I am Sir Henry Richmond, and I hail from London, where, if Mr Courthope ever finds himself I shall do my best to improve the friendship which has commenced in this unlooked for way.'

And thus were brought together by the

decree of fate, or in obedience to the law which had been set going from the beginning of things, these four persons, whose after lives were intertwined and commingled for the end and purpose of elucidating a great mystery and for the enlightenment and profit of mankind.

CHAPTER III

JAMES LAYTON (as Geoffrey afterwards learnt) was a merchant who had made a fortune in the Australian trade, and was wise enough to know when he had enough of wealth. So he had left his great business and his successful speculations, and while yet in middle age deemed it a healthier, and certainly, to a man of his tastes and affections, a more ennobling pursuit, to travel with his only child, with the intention of eventually making a home in England. He was a widower; his much-loved wife had been taken from him after a few short years of cherished companionship, leaving to his care their daughter, the sole remaining object of her father's great love — and Doris was altogether worthy of her parent's affection. She had grown into womanhood, as beautiful in mind as in person. Of a sweet and tender nature, her father's love had shielded her from every care; and now, at the age of nineteen, she was a bright and lovable woman, of a happy disposition, yet with a trace of seriousness in her face which fitly became its dark and dreamy beauty. She was tall and, by strangers, might have been considered cold, but not so by those who had the privilege of her friendship, who knew something of the depths of her nature— of the warmth of her affection, and of her bright intelligence and sound common sense. She had been well and healthily educated; her thoughts were innocent, and her day dreams were maidenly, with a hint of something akin to poetry and romance in them. Those who looked into her dark eyes could see, if they had the power to read the truth, the sweet and candid soul imprisoned and waiting for its deliverer — a Sir Galahad, or, perhaps, a Sir Lancelot (who could tell?)—who would release it and impart to it the knowledge which as yet it had not acquired. As for Sir Henry Richmond, his history may soon be told. A young Englishman of large estate, who had inherited his baronetcy, his good physique and his intellectual capacity from his father.

He had been educated in the usual way of Englishmen. From Eton he passed to Cambridge, and took a good degree there. His predilections were mathematical, and his pastimes were of the athletic order. He was in the first Cricket Eleven, and was not undistinguished on the river. He was called from College to witness the death-bed scene of his father. He fell naturally into the routine of the life of an English country gentleman.

The head of his family, he lived at his country seat, presided over by his mother with some amount of state, and certainly with dignity. He rode and shot well, but apart from the exercise afforded by the one, and the obligations which the other pursuit required of him, he was not particularly devoted to horses or to the slaughter of birds. He was of studious habits, and was more often to be found in the splendid library of Fleckton Hall, among its books, than in the park, among its noble beeches. Poetic and sentimental in tastes, the river, which ran for miles through his estate, claimed more of his attention, for he loved the mild excitement of trout fishing (the contemplative man's delight), and the quietude of natural objects fed his mind with sympathetic and sweet suggestions.

This poetic nature had a tinge of melancholy in it, and a leaning to mysticism, with a desire to pierce the veil of the unknown—to pry into the mystery of life and of the future of the race—not so much by scientific treatment as from the side of sentiment and feeling. The elucidation of occult meanings, and the observation of phenomena appearing on the borderland of being, occupied his mind. He recognised the reign of unalterable law, while he was a devout believer in the special guardianship and love of the Omniscient Lawgiver.

Henry Richmond, in the course of his omnivorous and desultory reading, had studied the works of Shakespeare with enthusiasm, and found in them not only the delight which arises from contemplating the beautiful, but much of hidden meaning which appealed to the mystic side of his nature. As 'adventures come to the adventurous,' so proofs of his peculiar aspect of things readily came to his hand in his search for them in the pages of the Poet of the Human Race; and he revered Shakespeare as a prophet with a message to man to be revealed at the time appointed.

CHAPTER IV

THE Laytons had only intended to remain in Chicago for a few days on their way through from San Francisco to Europe—for they had chosen the longer route from Melbourne, by way of Japan and the sea voyage across the Pacific, in order to take the World's Fair on their way; but the meeting, under such exciting circumstances, with Geoffrey Courthope brought about a much longer stay. That young gentleman, with true American hospitality, insisted on doing the honours of the city, and would, if he could have had his way, have put them all up at his beautiful house. As it was he had to be content with the company of Sir Henry, in whom he soon found a kindred spirit. The two men had similar tastes, and had each travelled much about the world. Sir Henry was then making his way to Guatemala and the Central American region, his curiosity excited by the description given him of the ruined monuments of a forgotten race buried in the thick forests of the interior. His desire was to translate the hidden secrets and ancient mysteries which might be contained in the wondrously carved stones of the ancient temples and monuments. Geoffrey, bent upon the solution of a more modern, but equally puzzling, problem, felt a strong sympathy for his new friend. Many evenings, before bedtime and after it, the two men interchanged ideas until it appeared probable that Geoffrey, fascinated by Richmond's account of the possibilities contained in the Central American forests, would accompany him there. Nevertheless, there were two influences at work, slowly at first, but with added strength as the days went by, which not only effectually checked such desire on Geoffrey's part, but stopped altogether Richmond's intended journey to Guatemala and caused him to turn towards the opposite direction.

Geoffrey's conversation on the Shakespeare

problem had highly interested Richmond. New views on the subject of the true author, confirmed by his own intimate knowledge of his works, somewhat undermined his faith in William Shakespeare and whetted his appetite for more information on the special subject which, up to now, had not excited much of his attention, while Geoffrey felt that the more he saw of the delightful Doris Layton the more his inclinations induced him to court her society; and what more agreeable way of doing so than by accompanying her and her father to England, with the ostensible object of another visit to Stratford-on-Avon to search further for such materials or evidence as he might find—a clue to which he believed he had obtained. Sir Henry's growing interest in the new subject, and his belief that he could render valuable aid to his friend, decided him to prolong his stay in Chicago, and, finally, to give up his original intention and to accompany him to England.

Geoffrey had taken upon himself the disposal of the time of his new friends while they were in the city. He planned and carried out many agreeable excursions and visits. But outside the World's Fair there was little to be seen; so as the weather was pleasant, and their own company decidedly the most agreeable, they left the crowded city, first travelling westward over the Illinois prairie lands to Rock Island on the Mississippi, and embarking on one of the high-pressure steamboats, peculiar to western rivers, for a trip to St Louis and back. On their return to Chicago they went up the lake in Geoffrey's steam yacht as far as Mackinaw, at its northern extremity, and as the summer was now advanced, this water journey was also a success.

The hospitality of the American, and his desire to be of service to his friends, were proffered in such a pleasant and delicate manner as to preclude the possibility of refusal. Remonstrance only produced from Geoffrey the assertion 'That he would not at all object to being taken about in the same way when he visited them in England, and that it was natural he should seek to make their stay in the States as agreeable as possible.' The result was that they accepted the situation and enjoyed themselves fully, mentally assuring themselves of the impossibility of sufficiently reciprocating the young American's attentions.

As the acquaintance of Doris and Geoffrey ripened, they became mutually attracted to each other. She expanded under his attentions, which were offered with delicacy and refinement, were so unmarked as to be quite unnoticeable by others, but in her secret soul she felt (yet was innocent of the cause) a growing sense of pleasure arise, which might hereafter blossom into love.

It would almost seem that Geoffrey possessed a special perception which enabled him to anticipate her desires, and she also found within herself an ability to divine his thoughts. They were, in fact, mentally *en rapport* from the very first, and probably their minds acted and re-acted upon each other when they were apart, as well as when they were near. This power, call it by the scientific name of psychology, or the more modern term telepathy, probably accounted for the vague and mysterious sense of a previous knowledge of each other, which had taken the shape, in Geoffrey's case, of the dream-face he beheld the night previous to the fire, and in her recognition of Geoffrey, on the same occasion, as of one whom she also had seen before.

CHAPTER V

THE graceful *Winona*, steaming swiftly northward through the early morning haze, parting the waters of Michigan with her sharp prow, was a sight to gladden the eye of a yachtsman. Of about 150 tons burthen, with raking masts and funnel, overhanging counter and faultless lines, she was acknowledged to be the handsomest and swiftest boat on the great lakes. As the sun rose higher, its rays lighted up the scene, showing the only land in sight, the green shores of Wisconsin on the left, with here and there a town or village, the tin-covered roofs of the houses glinting in the sun. On the blue waters of the lake, and through the golden haze, were seen floating the picturesque sailing boats waiting for the wind, and now and then the noisy and ugly propellers of cargo steamers churning their way to their destinations.

The first to appear on the saloon deck was Geoffrey, who glanced around, first towards the shore, to make out the position of the *Winona*, and then at his ship, with pardonable pride. Soon a quiet smile of content appeared on his handsome face, and a softened look was in his eyes. He felt happy—very happy. He possessed health, youth and wealth, and his dark-eyed Doris was near him, to whom as yet he had made no further declaration of his feelings than by signs which might have touched lightly, as a zephyr touches, the sensitive soul of the maiden.

Henry Richmond joined his friend, and they paced up and down, drawing in the fresh morning air with enjoyment.

'Tell me something,' said Richmond, 'about our port of destination, this Mackinaw—a name, by-the-bye, of no means pleasant sound—Indian, I suppose. You Americans have retained some very sweet survivals, such as Erie, Ontario, Illinois, Wisconsin, Winona and so forth; but Chicago, Milwaukee, Oshkosh, Osaukie, Pawtucket, Mackinaw, are indefensible. Who was poor Tucket? And was his poverty a reason that he should be remembered?'

'At least,' said the other, 'such names are infinitely better than the names that might have been Jacksonville, Tompkinsville or Red-dog, and hundreds of others neither beautiful nor useful. Probably these ugly names may have their effect upon the people who reside in such afflicted places; and if, by chance, a child born in one of them were to develop into a genius it would be an unpleasant fact for his biographer to admit that the subject of his memoir was born in the town of Red-dog.'

'Probably,' said Richmond, 'the influence of names on individuals has not yet received due attention. To me, names convey indications of character as well as personality. Richard gives me the idea of a weak man, fair and small; Robert is strong, dark and robust; and who can tell but that a name given to a child may influence his career? Or, it may be, that cause and effect are reversed, and in obedience to some unknown law the name has been given to the child because the after man could be none other than strong or weak, dark or fair. Consider feminine names: the stately, dark and languorous Eleanor; the lively, fair Beatrice—and her name reminds me how aptly the names of Shakespeare's heroines fit their characters and personalities. The genius of the Poet applies here as well as elsewhere, for he could not have done otherwise than appropriate beautiful names to his beautiful women. Do you know the name of Lady Macbeth?'

'No,' said Geoffrey.

'You won't find it in the play. It was Gruoch, a distinctly harsh name, though suitable to a murderess. But Shakespeare has made her sufficiently abhorrent without introducing the further painful fact of her unlovable name.'

'But how about the exceptions? I have known a Lily five feet eleven high, one hundred and sixty pounds in weight, and with a Roman nose; a Juno—her father is a pork packer in my native city — who is thin to transparency, very much under the middle height, and possesses an absolutely expressionless face. The cook of the *Winona* is one of the numerous Washingtons.'

'I treat your exceptions in the usual way; besides, Washington suggests one of the cook's employments.'

'Or, in other words,' said Geoffrey, 'all Washingtons should develop into statesmen or cooks.'

By this time Mr Layton had ascended from his stateroom and joined the others. He remarked,—

'I don't know how it may affect your extremely learned arguments, but I once knew a romantic couple, a Mr and Mrs Rose—his horticultural name may have been one of the reasons why she married him — whose first children, twin girls, the parents in the excess of their romanticism named Wild and Briar. When the boys came they also had appropriate names. One, I remember, was Marshal Niel. The neighbours suggested Dog for the fifth boy, but the name was not appreciated. However, I am only concerned with the fortunes of the elder of the twins. When she grew into womanhood and beauty everyone said, "What a delightfully suitable name," and Wild Rose was sought in marriage by young Mr Astor—no relation to the millionaire, for he was a clerk in a dry goods store at thirty shillings a week. Still everyone said, "How delightfully suitable, Wild Astor, you know." Then Mr Bull, the rich contractor, came along and married her, with a result which I leave you to guess—whether or not her new name influenced her disposition I cannot say, but Mrs Wild Bull has, I hear, displayed a violent temper ever since her marriage.'

Whatever other stories Layton, Richmond and Geoffrey might have had ready for the occasion were stayed by the announcement of breakfast, and the three adjourned to the saloon, to find Doris already there with her morning greeting — affectionate for her father, frankly friendly for Sir Henry, and friendly, with some amount of shyness, for Geoffrey. She presided at the breakfast table by right, and soon the conversation was resumed in the half-serious, half-humorous style as before.

'We have been discussing a very serious question on deck,' said Layton to his daughter, 'and probably you can assist us. Richmond maintains that names influence character, and Courthope says that character influences names. You may dissent, Courthope, and perhaps I have not got it right, but you will admit you disagreed with Sir Henry. They each gave some fine proofs; I only told them a tale.'

'Before Miss Layton gives us the benefit of her opinion,' said Sir Henry, 'it is only fair to let her know something more about the matter,' and he went over it briefly for her benefit; but he got much mixed and, somehow, found himself ardently advocating the other side of the question.

Geoffrey ventured to interpose, and was promptly sat on by Richmond and Layton, until the meeting was called to order by Doris, who said, 'This important subject seems to have been misunderstood altogether. The point has been missed of the meaning as well as the sound in names. A name may be pretty to the ear, while its meaning may be unbeautiful, or a sweet-meaning name may be ugly in sound, therefore, if you will kindly re-argue the case with this in view, whatever attention I can spare from my breakfast I will give to it.'

'O wise young judge, how I do honour thee!' murmured Geoffrey.

This new view of the case broke up the discussion, and other subjects were introduced. An adjournment took place to the deck where, under an awning, they ranged themselves in chairs and lounges. Geoffrey pointed out the various objects familiar to him. The high-banked passenger steamers passed. Flags were dipped and whistles blown in salute to the graceful *Winona*. The weather was delightful, and nothing marred the pleasure of the journey. As their time was their own, they called in at more than one port on the Wisconsin shore, or, what was more delightful, steamed at half-speed through the starlit night and made a veritable summer voyage of it.

The close relationship which the circumscribed limits of a yacht induced between the voyagers developed an increased warmth of friendship and esteem. Layton exhibited a heartiness and humour which added much to the good spirits of the party, and his tales of adventure and success in the Colonies were always welcome. He regarded the two younger men with equal interest and affection. As a man of worldly knowledge, he fully understood the possibilities included in their association with his daughter ; but he felt that one day she would surely fulfil her mission as a woman, and if either of his two friends, who, to his mind, were equally meritorious, should be lucky enough to become his son-in-law, his

Doris would indeed be happy. When such thoughts came to him, he remembered his own brief happiness, and he felt that she who had made those few years so full of peace and love would approve of his conduct.

As yet he saw in Doris no sign of preference for either; but there was one of the party who, with a perception rendered more sensitive by an incipient desire of his own, felt, rather than saw, signs of the growing sympathy between Doris and Geoffrey. It was Sir Henry, who, with a fine sense of honour, repressed any growing sentiment he possessed in favour of the friend to whom he owed his life. His bearing was that of a *Preux Chevalier* in thought as in deed.

CHAPTER VI

APPROACHING the higher latitude of the head of the lake, the *Winona* neared the Michigan shore, which is of a more rugged character than the western side, and steamed slowly up the coast towards the Straits. Our party were as usual assembled on deck, in lazy enjoyment of the fine weather — the men smoking, Doris reading a book and occasionally joining in the conversation. She had selected Shakespeare from the yacht's library. She found it to be annotated in writing, which she suspected was that of Geoffrey Courthope; and he was not loth to admit the fact. She was a ready and appreciative listener, and her clear and receptive mind absorbed and understood his explanations.

He told her of his admiration for the

works, and the interest he took in the elucidation of their authorship problem, and soon attracted the attention of the others, who joined in to form an intellectual symposium in which serious controversy was tempered with jokes. No theory was too absurd. Attack and defence changed sides. The really profound knowledge of the subject possessed by Richmond and Courthope was admirable. Parallelisms were discussed, and an attempt was made to prove logically that Shakespeare never existed, but that, if he did, he, and not Bacon, must have written the *Novum Organum*. *The Great Cryptogram* was cited; and Layton undertook to give, by the same method, a history of the voyage of the *Winona* from the Play of *Hamlet*, and so the ball was kept rolling.

Doris was as usual regarded as the judicial authority, and her mind was much exercised by what she heard. Beneath the surface of the subject there appeared a vein of significant circumstance which aroused her curiosity. The treatment of the matter was new to her, and savoured of irreverence. With a desire for information, she ventured to say,—

'It would indeed be desirable to clear the character of Shakespeare from the charge of literary fraud, and prove the falsity of such attacks. Shakespeare and his poetry are so associated that it is painful to me, as it must be to thousands, to be disillusionised, or even to have the slightest doubt cast on his fame.'

'If ever the true author be discovered,' said Geoffrey, 'it will be but the transference of your admiration, Miss Layton, to a more worthy object.'

'And when such discovery is made, if it ever will be,' said Sir Henry, 'the irritation of the mind, caused by suspicion, will pass away, and we shall be free to venerate the author with a full and complete assurance that our worship is given at the true shrine.'

'I don't share your views,' said Layton. 'I am satisfied to have my Shakespeare without being curious about the author. It's a matter of indifference to me who wrote Shakespeare — whether it was he, Francis Bacon, or anyone else. I think it was Charles Lamb who said, "The Plays of Shakespeare were not written by Shakespeare, but by another man of the same name." It is all the same to me.'

'But you must admit, papa, you would not encourage a fraud.'

'Ah! now you've got me. You have awakened my slumbering sense of justice; and if your Shakespeare turns out to be the wrong Shakespeare, I will have him prosecuted according to law.'

'Or public opinion,' said Richmond.

'*Fiat justitia*, etc,' said Geoffrey.

'What a noble quest it would be,' said Doris, 'to find out the truth!'

'We will do it,' chorussed the men.

'How?' said Doris.

'That remains to be hereafter decided,' remarked the chorus.

'Dinner is ready,' said the chief steward; and they went down to the saloon.

CHAPTER VII

THE *Winona* was safely moored alongside the wharf at Mackinaw Island that evening.

It was carried unanimously by our friends that they should go ashore and inspect the place there and then, especially as the starshine was unusually bright. The village presented few attractions. The noble Red Indian was represented by a few dilapidated and degenerate specimens, who offered for sale beaded moccasins and other useless articles as their own work; but they were probably turned out and distributed from some factory in the States at a much cheaper rate of production than would have been possible by the Indian Squaw. Such are the benefits of centralisation. They went through the principal street and back again.

'Mackinaw is deficient in beauty,' said Layton.

'Except when the *Winona* is here,' replied Richmond.

Leaving the village, they ascended the hill at the back. The path led to the Fort, about two hundred feet above the lake. Once upon a time Mackinaw was in the wilderness, beyond the limits of civilisation, and a frontier fortification had been built for defence against the Indians. On the delimitation of the boundary line between the Dominion of Canada and the United States the Fort of Mackinaw was retained *en garde* as a defensive work, with a company of United States troops in camp; but our friends met no one on the road. The evening was calm and still. The bright, beautiful stars above seemed nearer than usual: their light passed through the pure air so brightly that one might have read by it. Fireflies and glowworms showed brightly their phosphorescent sparks, and, as a contrast, the country away to the south was lighted up by the red-and-yellow flames of a great forest fire. Soon the friends passed the postern gate of he Fort, and were much surprised when the challenge of the sentry reminded them that they were trespassing. The guard turned out and surrounded the party. The Commandant appeared with due military severity at the possibility of a Canadian raid; but this changed to the most polite and amiable manner when he found out who his visitors were. The guard was then turned in again, and the Fort made free to our friends.

This little episode was the source of much amusement, and an invitation to the Commandant to dinner the next day on the *Winona* having been proffered by Geoffrey, and duly accepted, the party took their leave.

Doris and Geoffrey this time led the way up the hill. Its steepness hardly suited Layton and his fifty years; and rather than mar the pleasure of his friends he suggested they should continue their walk and he would sit by the pathside until their return.

Richmond declared he also was tired, and would remain with Mr Layton; and it may be said that if the former were not strictly truthful in his remark it was from no selfish cause. So Doris and Geoffrey went on alone.

The circumstances making up the lives of

men and women are due to external causes, or, as a Dutch philosopher illustrated it, 'We are so many cheeses rolling down a hill.' Some arrive safely at the bottom, some come to an untimely end in the beginning, some in the middle of the descent, others unite, with more or less cohesion, and travel together to the end. The roundness of the cheeses, the gradient of the hill, the obstructions, stones, ruts and roughnesses of the path, are so many influences at work ; and the contact of two cheeses coming together, with a touch and effect, varying from the soft alighting of a butterfly on a flower, to the force and consequence of an earthquake, is a more or less good illustration of one of the most important events in the lives of men and women. It may be observed that cheeses are round — that is, circular, not necessarily spherical—and that cheeses represent the classes, from the lordly Camembert down to the plebeian Gouda ; but they are all going the same road. These conscious cheeses, impelled by environing forces, move, act and have their being. Some are thoughtful, and ask themselves and each other questions about the journey and their destination ; others philosophise, and conclude that, although the journey is down hill, there is surely rest at the bottom. There may be those who say, 'We will take a course of our own,' and may vainly think they are directing themselves; but the result is the same: they break down on the way, or arrive at the end like the others. But the hill of life and the human cheeses, and the law of gravitation they obey, are the creation of Immortal Providence.

Doris of Melbourne and Geoffrey of Chicago walked side by side, with the novel feeling that they were alone. There was an acute sensitivity, or receptive ability, in each which required no word expression. They were silent. The night was beautiful and without sound, except what an acute ear might have detected in the subworlds of life. The odours of the pine forest scented the air, and the stars looked down with gleaming eyes. But a few weeks ago they were strangers, and now, through fine filaments, less materialised than thought itself, they spoke their love. By a process of the soul they comprehended each other. Their footsteps ended— she with downcast looks, he seeking through lids, and eyes beneath, down into her being for a sign, until the tension was too much to bear. 'Doris, sweet Doris!' he murmured; and she, in a voice like the impression given by a tender, delicate colour, whispered back his name.

CHAPTER VIII

THE tranquillity and happiness of our friends on board the *Winona* were increased by the new relationship of Doris and Geoffrey. Mr Layton, regarding the matter from a parental point of view, made no secret of his pleasure, stipulating for as much of his daughter's love and society as heretofore—at least, for some time to come. Richmond offered his congratulations with the warmth of a brother, and with a wee bit of feeling in a corner of his heart that, while the momentous event was the accomplishment of his dearest wish, the 'what might have been' would have made a great difference in his life. But he suppressed the thought with the loyalty of a chivalrous man.

After a few days stay at Mackinaw, to take

in coal and supplies, it was decided to run through the Straits into Lake Huron and take a peep at the dominions of Her Majesty, Queen Victoria. So, passing the entrance of the St Marie river, which leads up to Lake Superior, they coasted the great Manitoulin Island, and sought on its tree-fringed shores a spot on which to land. The *Winona* was stopped opposite the mouth of a creek. The cutter was manned, our friends were rowed to a shelving beach, and a landing was effected. The rugged character of the island, its immense pine forests and its sombre appearance, well becomes the horror in which it was held in olden times by the Indian tribes. They regarded it as the abode of spirits and avoided it. If driven, by stress of weather, to land thereon, they sought to propitiate the Manitou by offerings of articles of clothing, which they hung to the trees. The belief in spiritual existence is the universal primitive religious motive. It may be explained naturally, but it is none the less providential in its origin and development.

However, the dreary character of the place did not affect the spirits of the party. A likely spot was selected, and an impromptu picnic was proceeded with. Mr Layton built the fire with sticks found by Geoffrey in the pine woods, Richmond brought water from the creek, and Doris made the tea. With Shakespearian thought intent, some resemblance was discovered to Prospero's Island. They could fit in the surroundings; and as for themselves, there were Miranda and Prospero. Geoffrey was naturally Ferdinand, by virtue of his new condition as lover of Doris; but what part was there for poor Henry Richmond? He was too solid for Ariel, and much too well-built and good-looking for Caliban. While they were merrily discussing the matter, out of the woods came an interruption in the form of a hunter, with his rifle and dogs, who, when he saw the party, made his way towards them. He was attired in serviceable clothes, suitable to the rough work of the forest. His muscular form and sunburnt face and hands denoted endurance and a life in the open air. As he approached, he lifted his cap with well-bred courtesy, and mutual greetings passed. At a glance it could be seen he was English and a gentleman. It is not the custom of the woods to be too ceremonious, and Geoffrey invited him to join them.

'What sport have you had?' said Layton, as a natural opening to conversation.

'I have shot nothing this morning,' replied the stranger, 'and am on my road back to camp. From the high land I saw your boat put off, and made my way down to the shore, curious to know the object of your arrival. I have been away from civilisation for so long a time that I could not resist the temptation of coming to you. This is my excuse.'

'It is not needed,' said Layton. 'The solitary life of a hunter in this uninviting island needs some change, and we quite understand your feelings.'

Doris handed a cup of tea to the guest—his plate was filled—and the conversation was taken up by Sir Henry, who had been regarding the stranger with a puzzled expression, when a sudden illumination of memory lighted up his face. He said,—

'Your living on this island will make your return to England all the more enjoyable. The contrast between the shady side of Piccadilly and the Manitoulin woods must give you a hankering after the less rugged life of the west end.'

'Yes,' was the rejoinder. 'I feel cut off from associations which have their delights; but the open air and independence are preferable.'

'Yet,' said Sir Henry, 'a rubber at the Marlborough, or Polo at Hurlingham, are pleasant; and knocking over the cock pheasants in the coverts at Fleckton, and landing a three-pound trout from the river there, are pleasures not to be despised.'

'Richmond, I see you recognise me,' said the stranger; 'but let my secret remain with you.'

Richmond for answer grasped his hand, and addressing his friends, said, 'Let me apologise for this demonstration. I have found in this gentleman a friend whom I thought I might never see again. His voluntary exile is caused, as I and his friends know, from a mistaken sense of duty on his own part. I can say no more; but I feel that the circumstances which have so cruelly told against him will be set right, and he will return to his proper position in society.'

'And until they are—' replied the stranger, 'for I shall not lift a finger or speak a word to alter them—I shall remain here, or in some other place, far from the world which has chosen to condemn me. I also apologise for this painful scene. Believe me, if I had known that Sir Henry Richmond was among you I should not have intruded, although the happiness of meeting him and finding that he does not doubt me is great indeed.

'I beg,' said Geoffrey, 'you will put yourself at ease. A single word of my intimate friend Richmond is enough. Whatever misfortune has overtaken you, I believe you do not deserve it, and I beg you will look upon me as being honoured by your presence to-day. Will you come with us? My yacht has room for you, and we shall be returning at once.'

'I am indeed grateful,' was the reply, 'but I cannot, and Sir Henry knows the reason of my inability; but, believe me, I am very thankful for your generosity and the kindness you all show me.'

And when the cutter went off with our friends, and the *Winona* steamed away, they waved adieu to the solitary figure on shore, and wondered whether they would ever see him again.

CHAPTER IX

THE voyage back to Chicago was pleasant, but uneventful. The *Winona* re-passed the Straits, coasted the Michigan shore, visiting some of the towns on the way, and crossed over to her port of Chicago.

It was natural that Doris and Geoffrey found increased delight in each other's society, and the close association of ship-board brought them nearer together; but they were unselfish enough not to mar the pleasure of the yachting voyage by devoting themselves entirely to their new position as engaged lovers. Mr Layton and Sir Henry Richmond had their full share of attention, and many were the pleasant discussions held by the four friends before the voyage ended. The beautiful weather, their high spirits, the happy engagement of Doris and Geoffrey, brought about a condition in the three younger members of the party nearly approaching enthusiasm, while the older, Mr Layton, felt a sober joy at the good fortune that was happening to render his life peaceful and contented. He even became as enthusiastic as the others on the subject of the Shakespeare problem! The stores of knowledge possessed by Geoffrey and Sir Henry were opened, and Doris imbibed information which she was prompt to receive and utilise. Her love for Geoffrey and her interest in the problem inclined her towards adherence to the inquiry which, in a grand council, was determined on. Their leisure and their wealth would give them opportunity and time—and what could not be done with these, supported by their sincerity and ardour? But in what direction should they work? When they arrived in England they would formulate a practical line of discovery. At present all was vague, and they only were aware of their ardent hopes and expectations.

Said Geoffrey 'Everything associated with Shakespeare—his Plays and Poems—the limited references of his contemporaries, the few concrete memorials left of him, have all been worn threadbare by examination, and the hunger for information has not been appeased. The most searching investigation into his life has produced many volumes, but the most meagre results; and such facts as have been unearthed relating to his father, his children and his occupations, negative the assumption of his claims as the learned creator of the Plays and Poems. Is it possible for the author of *Hamlet* to have allowed his daughter to go through life ignorant of reading and writing? And yet Shakespeare's daughter Judith was in such condition. This fact alone throws discredit upon the inference that William Shakespeare was himself a man of extraordinary learning, or of that great humanity such as the author of the Plays must have been. Indeed, the scholarship of the true author is the chief argument against William Shakespeare's claim. Ben Jonson says, "He had little Latin and less Greek." Yet the *Comedy of Errors* is in a great measure taken from the *Menæchini* of Plautus, and there was no English translation as old as his time; therefore, the writer of the *Comedy of Errors* was a Latin scholar, which Shakespeare was not. Besides, the author was acquainted with Italian and French, and it is absurd to suppose that Shakespeare's education included the acquisition of these languages. The evidence of these facts is made abundantly clear by the writers of Shakespeare's life, among whom Halliwell Phillipps stands foremost. His *Outlines of the Life of Shakespeare* is a wonderful monument of the author's zeal, and contains absolutely everything known of Shakespeare, his family and his works.'

'I have read the book,' said Richmond, 'with admiration, and I have also read Donnelly's *Great Cryptogram*, which, apart from the mysterious and fantastical cipher narrative in the second volume, is a remarkable and painstaking argument in favour of Francis Bacon as the true author. I think he goes far to disprove Shakespeare's claim, but not far enough to prove that of Bacon. When it is remembered that the great Chancellor's controlling desire was self-advancement at all risks, that he took bribes, that he debased his position as a judge by selling judgments, and was guilty of acts which drew upon him from Pope the unenviable distinction of being the "meanest of mankind," it is, to say the least, extremely improbable that he possessed the nobility of thought, the purity of sentiment and the genius, which touches the heart while it inspires the soul, possessed by the true author.'

'And yet,' said Doris, 'it must have been he—for, by the exhaustive process, if it were not Shakespeare, then who but Bacon could it have been? There was no one else in the sixteenth century capable. Marlowe, Spenser, Jonson, Raleigh, all lived at the time; but none of them were capable of such greatness.'

'Perhaps, who knows,' remarked Layton, 'some unknown author may yet be discovered, who lived in poverty and died unknown, labouring for a pittance, coining from the mint of his brain the golden thoughts which move and thrill the hearts of men for all time.'

'The same idea has occurred to me,' replied Geoffrey. 'But, instead of the indigent poet, I can conceive the existence of a man, neither Bacon nor Shakespeare, but of so powerful a brain, of so great an intellect, of such vast learning and experience of the world and mankind, as to have been head and shoulders above the people of his day—a very demi-god in wisdom and knowledge, who lived within himself, indifferent to the praise or blame of his fellow creatures, having a pride in his intellectual powers which rendered him contemptuous of the whole world—a grand solitary figure, like a single lofty mountain in a flat country—an individuality which stood alone, erect, god-like and unapproachable. A personality of this unique capacity, whose ability to acquire knowledge and impart wisdom was miraculous, permitted himself to give forth his finest thoughts for the happiness of man. His brain yielded creations wiser, nobler, more prophetic, sweeter and more beautiful than those of the ancient authors, philosophers and poets; but while he was willing that his fellowmen for all time should be made happier and better by his works, his very greatness and nobility elevated him to the lofty position from which he looked down, silent in his pride, and regardless of fame.'

'A dream! my dear fellow, a dream!' said Layton.

And a dream it remained.

CHAPTER X

FLECKTON HALL is a modern mansion house—the central figure of a large landed estate in the south of England—the patrimony of the Richmond family for many past generations. Fleckton is remarkable for its splendid woods, its spacious park of oaks and elms, and the great house built by the present baronet's father in the Tudor style. It was more Tudor in its modern, but correct, treatment than any existing sixteenth century house. Its red brick and white stone exterior was a distinguishing mark for miles, while it commanded, from its elevation on the side of the South Downs, a glorious view over wood and vale to the distant Channel. Although the manor of Fleckton contained a fairly large acreage, divided into farms, with solid houses and buildings, the property was more of a pleasure domain than a source of income. The Richmonds were in the happy position of being rich without reference to their lands. Marriages with wealthy heiresses, who had brought money into their hands, and more than all, a judicious investment in consols at the critical period before the battle of Waterloo, had been the means of the formation of a fund, the income of which was ample enough to place the family among the richest in England. The gardens of Fleckton were remarkable. Sir Henry's father had been a great lover of trees and plants, and had formed the gardens into divisions of countries, with vegetation appropriate to each. The soil of the several countries had been brought there, from Italy, Egypt, India, Spain, China and other places, so that the transplanted trees and plants might thrive and feel at home. With appropriate backgrounds and accessories, the pictures thus presented were curious and instructive. Most quaint was the representation of 'the willow pattern plate' in the Chinese garden, with the temple, the willow trees, the canal and the bridge: all were there, but the little men crossing over.

And similarly one could wander through the other gardens, and visit each country in turn without the inconveniences and expense of travelling. These studied artificialities had their contrast in the Wild Garden of several acres, wherein all kinds of English wild flowers grew, and through which dashed a miniature torrent, with here and there a quiet pool overflowing into a cascade, and falling at last into the trout stream in the vale. The glories of the Winter Garden, covered with half an acre of glass, and filled with palms, fountains and statuary ; the spaciousness of the Riding School ; the delights of the Dairy—a Gothic Temple, all marble and glazed tiles, within whose cool and shaded depths the cult of cream and the belief in the best of butter were practised, were some of the prominent features of this stately English home, in which were now assembled the chief persons of our story. They had all arrived in England together, and Sir Henry Richmond had invited his three friends to Fleckton on a visit which promised to be of some duration.

Lady Richmond, Sir Henry's mother, the Châtelaine of Fleckton, until her son should bring home a wife, received him and his guests with that warmth they so well deserved, and with that gratitude to Geoffrey, due to him as the preserver of her son's life. To Doris she extended a motherly affection, inexpressibly touching, and a delightfully sympathetic attachment grew up between the two—the older lady interesting herself in the fortunes and the love of the younger, while she, motherless and unguided up to now by a friend of her own sex, regarded Lady Richmond with respectful and grateful devotion.

And so the days passed smoothly on into the autumn of the year. The house party was increased as the shooting season came, and the business of pleasure was in full swing. A series of entertainments were given by the Richmonds, not only in their capacity as leaders of county society, but in honour of Doris, her father and Geoffrey. The beautiful Australian, as the fiancée of the American millionaire, was accepted as a highly interesting and attractive girl, whose engagement to the man who had saved her life was voted a natural sequence of so romantic an episode. She was happy in the love which surrounded her, in the excitement of new associations and new people, and she could always fly from the crowd with Geoffrey to the comparative solitude of the library, or to the gardens or park, where alone they could indulge in those happy conversations which are so delightful to lovers.

There was no formality in the life at Fleckton. Guests could do pretty much as they pleased. Breakfast was on the table till very late in the morning. Lunch was served at hours varying with the moods and occupations of those who required it. The time for afternoon tea was supposed to be at five o'clock; but the dinner hour was more rigidly observed. All could do as they liked during the day; and those who were for out-door amusement might say, 'It is a fine day: let us kill something!' which meant death to the pheasant, the partridge and the rabbit; and those who preferred milder pleasures in or out of doors were free to indulge in them; but all were expected to meet at dinner, and invariably it was a pleasant rendezvous.

Wealth can command a good cook, but it requires a refined discrimination to select worthy guests—those who have the ability to talk well, and those with a capacity of listening well.

There is as much credit to the man or woman who can be 'silent in several languages' as to those who keep the ball of conversation rolling. Then again, it is often found that clever people are not always good-looking. It is a way Nature has of balancing things. And good-looking people are just as necessary to human happiness as witty ones, especially if you have to sit opposite them for an hour or two at dinner.

Now Lady Richmond possessed the art of selection of the right people for her house and dinner parties — the clever, the good-looking, the distinguished, and those who should amuse and interest the others who ought to be thus entertained; but all were incapable of *gaucheries* or of bad taste. In the Talmud there is among other wise maxims this one: 'Never say in the house of a man whose father has been hanged, "Hang up this fish for me;"' and doubtless the Rabbis, when they gave dinner parties, carefully eliminated from their list of invited guests those whose fathers had been hanged, and those likewise who might be guilty of alluding to such unpleasant circumstance. So at Lady Richmond's table one was sure to meet the most agreeable people. She drew the line in accordance with her own taste, and it sometimes was influenced more by her worldly wisdom than by her charity.

'Mother,' said Sir Henry one day in her boudoir, when they were discussing the next batch of guests to be invited to Fleckton, 'we never see anything of the Ellerslies. Linda must be out by this time. I remember her two years ago as a very sweet girl. Why not invite her, with her father and mother?'

'I don't see very well how we can have them here,' replied Lady Richmond, 'after the terrible misfortune that has happened in their family.'

'What misfortune do you mean? What has happened, mother?'

'Only what you already know,' said she. 'The stigma of their son's misdeeds rests upon all of them, and I have been obliged to erase them from my visiting list.'

'But surely you are too severe. The charge has never been proved against Rupert. I among many others never did believe him guilty. Appearances, I know, were against him; but I was his intimate friend at school and at college and afterwards also, and I know him to be incapable of dishonourable practices.'

'Then, why did he leave the country if he did not feel himself guilty?'

'He should never have done so if I had been in England at the time. He should have faced the charges and have defied proof. He, doubtless, was overwhelmed with the horror of the accusation, and, sensitive as he is, the very suspicion of such a charge as cheating at cards was enough to prostrate him and render him incapable of defending himself. If I had been by his side it would have been different. I shall run over to the Ellerslies to-morrow and tell them so. Moreover, I can give them the latest news of Rupert, for I met him in Canada; and they will be glad to see me under such circumstances, although it may have appeared to them that both you and I condemn their son for a crime which I feel sure, my dear mother, he never committed.'

'Be it so, Henry; and when the cloud of suspicion has been dispersed I shall be among the first to call on the Ellerslies.'

'I feel,' said Sir Henry, 'that I have left

poor Rupert's cause too long disregarded. I will at once take the matter up and try to clear his name. After I have seen the Ellerslies I shall go to town and look into the matter.'

'And where did you meet Rupert Ellerslie?' inquired Lady Richmond. 'And how was he looking?'

'By a remarkable circumstance we met him on an island, called the Great Manitoulin, in Lake Huron. We were cruising in the *Winona*—Courthope's yacht—and had landed on the desert shore. We were having afternoon tea, all of us—Geoffrey, Miss Layton and Mr Layton—when a hunter came out of the woods and approached our party, which he was invited to join. He was a handsome, bearded fellow, tall and sunburnt; but notwithstanding his changed appearance I knew him. He recognised me, of course. There was somewhat of a scene between us, which I had to excuse and explain so far as I might. I begged him to return and face the charge, but he told me he would make no effort to remove the impression. He seemed proud and indifferent, but beneath, no doubt, his heart was breaking. I will defend him. I will clear him.'

'Do so, Henry; and, if you like, I will call on the Ellerslies with you.'

'No, mother, not yet. I think it better, at least for the present, that I should work alone.'

CHAPTER XI

CARRYING out his intention, Henry Richmond left Fleckton next day in his dog-cart for the station, and went by rail, about twenty miles, to Southchester, near which place lived the Ellerslie family.

They were county people of good lineage and substance. Ellerslie Court—an ancient Elizabethan house of great beauty and size— had been their home for many generations. Now and then an Ellerslie was returned to Parliament, or filled the office of sheriff, or was chairman of Quarter Sessions; but their lives were not eventful; and certainly no stain had ever tarnished the family honour or name until, in this present generation of the Ellerslies, a great blow had fallen upon them. Suddenly an accusation had been made against Rupert,

the only son of the house, of card cheating
at his club. His indignant denial was useless
against the evidence of certain cards he produced
from his pockets, apparently to his own great
astonishment. Irregularities had been noticed
in the play, and suspicion had fallen upon a
player, whose antecedents, at least at cards, had
been somewhat suggestive. He had been more
than ordinarily lucky at critical moments, when
the stakes were unusually large, and on this
occasion there was no doubt in the mind of
everyone present (including that of a very
distinguished personage who was at the table),
that a substitution of cards had been made.
The person suspected was invited to empty
his pockets, which he promptly did, without
the result expected. 'Perhaps,' said someone,
'we had all better do the same,' which was
agreed to; and several useful cards of special
value at particular moments in the game they
were playing, were produced by Rupert. This
unexpected result was astounding. The con-
sternation was universal; but there was no gain-
saying facts, and Rupert shrank, horror-stricken
at the terrible proof which he was unable to
explain, while protesting his innocence. It was

hard to believe him, and opinion was divided regarding his conduct. From a club scandal, the matter became a public one; and Rupert, unable to disprove his apparent guilt, and proud in the knowledge of his own honour, chose self-exile rather than a further experience of the social injustice of which he was the victim.

Sir Henry walked out to Ellerslie Court from Southchester station. From the keeper at the lodge entrance he learned that the family were at home. So he proceeded up the avenue of limes to the house. Passing the fish ponds, he cut across the park by a path he remembered as a shorter way, and put up a herd of fallow deer, reclining among the bracken. They moved off slowly, as if unused to disturbance, and looked back with mild eyes at the stranger.

Making her way towards the Court, but in a direction at right angles to Sir Henry, was a lady; and as they approached each other, he wondered who she was.

In a minute or two he was near enough to see she was a slim, but graceful girl, dressed in grey cloth, with a cap of the same material half concealing her chestnut hair.

Notwithstanding the studious nature of Sir Henry, he had an eye for beauty, and he thought to himself, 'What a lovely girl!'

Just then a tall deerhound, which had been walking by the side of his mistress, looking up to her every now and then, with eyes that showed pride in being her protector, came bounding forward to Sir Henry with a menacing growl, which turned into a whine of pleasure when he reached him.

'What, Colonel! good Colonel!' said he as he recognised the animal, 'is it you? and Colonel's mistress too!' he continued. 'Linda, Miss Ellerslie, I should hardly have known you; you have grown out of knowledge. How do you do? You remember me?'

'Yes! You are Sir Henry Richmond,' she replied. 'Papa and mamma will be glad to see you; and yet—'

'Ah, well! I have brought you all the latest news of Rupert. I have met him abroad; and I shall be welcome, shall I not? They will be glad to see me, I am sure.'

'Indeed they will. Poor Rupert!' said Linda, 'tell me all about him, or wait until I run in and announce the good news.'

Richmond was welcomed by Mr and Mrs Ellerslie, who, borne down by the trouble of their only son's misfortune, but strong in their belief in his truth and honour, were only too anxious to hear of him.

Sir Henry told them of his finding their son in Canada alive and well; and he gladdened the parent's hearts by expressing his faith in his friend's innocence and his determination to unravel the mystery. This was the first gleam of happiness they had experienced since Rupert's departure, and amid their tears, the mother and daughter looked upon Sir Henry as a messenger of consolation, who might succeed in redeeming the character of Rupert. The father grasped his hand in silence, the mother blessed him, and the lovely Linda regarded him through her earnest blue eyes with an eloquence of admiration which could not be mistaken, and which was not lost upon the susceptible heart of Sir Henry.

To look at Linda was to love her; and as he appeared to her a knightly hero, the incense of her faith in him increased his ardour to bring to her side a brother freed from the stain of dishonour, not only for Rupert's sake, but that he might claim a reward from her—a guerdon which seemed to him too great for any task he might undertake.

Who could help loving Linda? sweet as the morning air in June, that lifts the roses and diffuses their fragrance! Beautiful as a Raphael Madonna, she had grown up within her father's house, unknown to the world, and restrained from society because of the blow which had fallen upon them. Her happy girlhood had developed into a lovely womanhood, whose perfection was unnoticed, even by her parents. A sweet saint of innocence and gladness, touched by present sorrow, and the more lovely for it, no wonder Sir Henry felt that, in the hope of winning her, he was earning his reward for his self-denial in having effaced his dawning love for Doris.

CHAPTER XII

AFTER partaking of the hospitality of the Ellerslies, Sir Henry left the Court loaded with the gratitude of the family; and, with promises on his part to return soon and to send them news of his movements, he returned to Fleckton to resume his position as host.

He told his mother all about his visit, omitting a too vivid description of Linda, but simply mentioning that she had grown considerably since he had seen her last.

There was no reason why Mr Layton, Doris and Geoffrey should not know that the stranger whom they had encountered on the Canadian island was Rupert Ellerslie, the heir of the Court, and the son of Sir Henry's friends; on the contrary, he felt that the outcome of their interest in him would be that they would seek his parents and, by their sympathy and friendliness, lighten the Ellerslie load of sorrow. Lady Richmond felt her heart melt at the account of Henry's visit to the Ellerslies, and was now as enthusiastic and warm in their favour as she had been reserved and cold before. She proposed to take the earliest opportunity of running over to the Court and of taking Doris with her. The way was paved by a letter from Sir Henry to Mr Ellerslie, asking what day would be convenient. A satisfactory reply was returned. Then commenced a series of visits on the part of Lady Richmond and Doris, accompanied afterwards by the three men, but the Ellerslies excused themselves from leaving their home.

An association of a very friendly kind grew up between the families of Fleckton and the Court, and more especially delightful was the affection between the two girls—the travelled and intellectual Doris, and Linda, the half-opened flower. The former very soon discovered the feeling that lay at the heart of Linda, the innocent adoration she had for Henry and her belief in him as a champion, who was to restore to her the lost brother. Doris noticed also, with a feminine instinct, the direction of Sir Henry's regard; she, therefore, clung closer to Linda with the love and watchfulness of an elder sister, while, in her gratitude and friendship, she lost no opportunity of encouraging the suit of Sir Henry.

As time went by, Sir Henry paid frequent visits to town to investigate the matter in which Rupert was concerned, to make the necessary inquiries, and to formulate a plan of discovery of the true facts relating to the card-cheating case. He was not very successful. Rupert and his supposed misdeed had been almost forgotten. Two years had elapsed; and it is a sufficiently long time in London society for a scandal to be forgotten, or, at least, to cease to remain of sufficient importance to be the subject of conversation. Besides, many other scandals had happened in the meantime, and only a vague recollection of the details of Rupert's case could be gleaned from Sir Henry's club friends, although, when his name was mentioned, they perfectly recollected its general features. They were, nevertheless, one and all, glad to hear that Sir Henry had met him abroad, and that he was in good health ; and the most distinguished personage of the club, with that kindliness of feeling and remembrance of individuals specially remarkable in him and his race, was so good as to make a particular inquiry about him, and to express to Sir Henry, as a confidential communication, his belief in Rupert's innocence, an assurance which was extremely gratifying and encouraging to listen to.

Many days passed, and nothing was done. The club was the same as usual. Men came and went, afternoon whist was played by the same coterie, high points and heavy betting were customary, games of chance were not interdicted by the rules, and gambling for big sums was not unusual. By inspecting the club registers Sir Henry found out the names of the members who were present on the evening so fatal to Rupert. He had conversed with most of them, at least with those whom he regarded as his friends, but gleaned only the fact that the suspected man had proved himself innocent and Rupert had shown himself guilty ; further than that he could not get. And how about the former ? Was he still a member of the club ?

No; he had taken his name off the books soon after the Ellerslie affair. He had been too lucky when large stakes were in question. He lost, it is true, sometimes, and complained much of his bad luck; but it was remarked that his ill-fortune occurred mostly when moderate play was taking place. Who was he? Sir Henry was told his name: one that was associated with the country's history. The bearer was of a noble house, whose members had done great things in their day. He was a younger son, and of comparatively small means. Membership of this particular club was accorded to the possessor of various qualifications: first, birth and wealth, then birth, and lastly, riches alone; but the riches must have been acquired in some irreproachable way. And one had to be very rich indeed, and willing to play five-pound points and fifties on the 'rub,' to be eligible.

Sir Henry made many inquiries as to the whereabouts of the man he sought, but none of his friends could give him any information. He had been met in Piccadilly and elsewhere occasionally, well-dressed, but having a dissipated appearance. No one knew to what club he now belonged, or his address, and as the

London *Directory* afforded no clue, Sir Henry, at length, sought the aid of a detective, who brought merely the negative information, that his whereabouts were unknown to the servants at the town house of his family.

Sir Henry made occasional flying visits to town, but each time returned no nearer to the object he had in view.

CHAPTER XIII

WHAT, it may be asked, had all this time become of the great Shakespearian problem? Was the quest forgotten? Were our friends so occupied by their pleasures, their loves and their employments, that they no longer remembered their resolve to search for the truth? No; they were as keen as ever, and amid the easy life at Fleckton, they frequently met together in the library and exchanged their views.

On the occasion of one of these discussions it was remarked by Mr Layton, 'We seem to have arrived in England with the intention of prosecuting a search. We set before our eyes an object to attain, an end to be gained; but, instead of working for our end, we have been, in this delightful house of Sir Henry, enjoying ourselves and taking our ease, and have advanced no further towards a practicable result. We have talked a great deal, but have done nothing. We might have remained in America for all the good we have done. Has any member of this highly intellectual, but unpractical, Shakespearian Society anything to suggest for the good of mankind in general, or this *dilettanti* body in particular?"

'It seems to me,' replied Sir Henry, 'that some move should be made. We have thrashed the matter out verbally and have decided most unanimously that something shall be done; but what?'

Said Doris, 'Did we not intend, as part of our programme, to visit Stratford and examine for ourselves the memorials of Shakespeare?'

'And that reminds me,' said Mr Layton, 'that you and I have never been to Stratford. It would be a good idea to take a trip there under Geoffrey's guidance.'

'In my mind,' said Geoffrey, 'it has always been a part of our programme to look up Stratford. I have a project which I have never yet hinted at, and which I cannot properly explain to you unless we are on the spot.'

'What is it, Geoffrey?' said Doris.

'It is certainly a bold scheme; but from the very first I have considered it the only practical and satisfactory one,' replied he. 'I would prefer to withhold an explanation until I have given it more thought, and have had another opportunity of making certain measurements and calculations necessary for its successful development.'

'You think you will find something new in the house in which Shakespeare was born?' asked Sir Henry.

'Or below it,' remarked Layton. 'There's a mysterious cellar. You want to get permission to dig below its floor for a secret vault or concealed receptacle, in which you may find manuscripts and other satisfactory matters?'

'Why not try New Place, where he lived?' said Sir Henry. 'You are more likely to find something by digging there. I am not at all sure that the owner may not have had a secret chamber in his house below the foundation, where he, for purposes of his own, concealed all his papers, especially those that related to the secret history of the plays he did *not* write.'

'Very likely,' drily replied Geoffrey; 'but you are on a wrong scent, my friends, although I cannot say your observations are not sagacious.' "You are getting warm," as the children say at hide-and-seek; 'but I am not prepared at present to say more. Wait till we are at Stratford, and then, if the circumstances be favourable, I will take you all into my confidence.'

At the first favourable opportunity; therefore, they left Fleckton for Stratford-on-Avon.

CHAPTER XIV

ARRIVED at the town, so celebrated as the place where William Shakespeare was born, where he lived for so many years, and where he died, our party put up at an hotel and made it their headquarters, from which they visited all places of interest in and around Stratford. They proposed to remain for several days, during which they diligently and patiently examined all the well-known buildings and objects of interest consecrated to the memory of the great dramatist.

As regards the house in which Shakespeare was born, Halliwell Phillipps observes, 'It must have been erected in the first half of the sixteenth century, but the alterations that it has since undergone have effaced much of its original character. Inhabited at various periods by tradesmen of different occupations, it could not possibly have endured without having been subjected to numerous repairs and modifications. The general form and arrangement of the tenement that was purchased in 1556 may yet, however, be distinctly traced, and many of the old timbers, as well as pieces of the ancient rough stone work still remain. There are also portions of the chimneys, the fireplace surroundings and the stone basement floor, that have been untouched, but most, if not all, of the lighter wood-work belongs to a more recent period. It may be confidently asserted that there is only one room in the entire building which has not been greatly changed since the days of the Poet's boyhood. This is the antique cellar under the sitting-room, from which it is approached by a diminutive flight of steps. It is a very small apartment, measuring only nine by ten feet.'

You may be sure that our friends paid particular attention to this sole surviving remnant of the sixteenth-century dwelling, and that they also visited and examined the remains of New Place with considerable interest and attention. Here, doubtless, were underground apartments and cellars necessary to a mansion of considerable importance; but, if they existed, they have not been found. 'Perhaps,' as it was suggested by Sir Henry, 'the truth may be preserved in New Place, and while the entire superstructure above ground has disappeared, with no record left regarding the reason for its demolition, there may be deep down, and purposely difficult of discovery, a secret chamber or muniment room whose treasures will hereafter see the light of day.'

'But this is only surmise,' said Layton. 'You have no facts to go upon.'

'It is only by theorising,' replied Sir Henry, 'that deductions are made. Besides, Phillipps admits that "there was at least one cellar in the Poet's day." The "at least" suggests the existence of more than one, and infers that a search may lead to the discovery of other underground apartments. None other than an examination of the superficial ground has been made, and I am surprised that, since the property has been vested in the Corporation of Stratford, a careful exploration of the ground below the surface, to a depth of at least twenty feet, has not been undertaken in the hope of making a discovery which may reveal a secret room in which Shakespeare, who lived on the site for years, may have deposited his records.'

'Well, there may be something in your theory; but what does Geoffrey say?' remarked Layton.

'I do not oppose any search in any new direction,' replied he. 'When the well-trodden path has led to a *cul-de-sac*, then we must make a way of our own — a road for ourselves — a short cut to the goal, not unattended by danger, and perhaps, also, by glory in the accomplishment of victory.'

'What do you mean, Geoffrey?' inquired Doris. 'I am sure you have some idea in your mind which you only hint at, and seem reluctant to impart. Do tell us all about it.'

'Not now, darling; but when we return to the hotel (this conversation was held at New Place) I will let you all know of my project, which, I may mention, I have been considering for some time; but it is of so startling a character, that I fear you may not support me.'

'That remains to be seen,' said Sir Henry. 'You excite my curiosity, and my apprehension too; but, rest assured, the bond which links me to you is strong enough to require that I shall follow and assist you, whatever the danger.'

'I shall reserve my decision,' said the more cautious Layton, 'until I hear from Geoffrey what his project amounts to.'

As for Doris, she looked at Geoffrey with eyes that eloquently spoke of faith and love.

CHAPTER XV

THAT evening, after dinner, Mr Layton, his daughter and Sir Henry prepared themselves to listen to Geoffrey's explanation of his great project to solve the Shakespearian mystery; and he addressed them as follows:—

'You all know, my friends, that the interest you take in this matter has been shared by me; or, to put it, I hope not too egotistically, the enthusiasm you exhibit has been caused by my initiative. The application I have been enabled to bring to the subject has developed a passion for the truth, in which you have participated, and my studies in the vast field of Shakespearian literature have increased my desire to elucidate a problem which that literature has classed among the great mysteries of the world. My own convictions have led me on the ambitious road to solve the problem, if possible, and I do not feel that any risk would be too great, or any sacrifice too severe, to attain my object. What I am about to propose to you will probably cause a shock to your moral perceptions, and may strike you as a bold and hazardous enterprise. I shall not be surprised at either result; and I foresee that it will require plenty of courage and energy to succeed. In regard to the moral aspect of the question, the sincerity of an act and the honesty of the actor should have some effect, and the equation of time some influence. I do not go so far as to say, " Do evil that good may come,"—although, by the way, it would be impossible and cruel to do otherwise in certain cases— but I say that there are circumstances which justify the commission of acts where a minor amount of, what some may denominate as wrong, shall be committed that "the right be done."

'The lesser evil must be committed to attain the greater good. There are great questions, which conscience only can answer—acts, the commission of which the law of the land would punish, but which to the conscience of the person committing them are right. History is full of such cases. Then again, if the common good is to be obtained, how much worthier is it to overcome obstacles with a courage equal to the purity of the motives impelling such action. The greater the risk, the greater the honour. I believe that, in what I am about to lay before you, I shall have your support, and I hope you agree with me that, in this instance, the end justifies the means.

'It is a matter of common knowledge that all that is discoverable has been discovered; in fact, nothing remains for further investigation: that is, the field of inquiry is limited, and the most minute and intense scrutiny has failed to yield further light on the subject. The materials have been worn threadbare, and nothing certain has been proved. It seems almost that the intention of the creator of the work has been to leave the question a doubtful, uncertain and insolvable puzzle for all time, or until it shall please him to reveal himself by the help of someone, possessed of courage and sagacity, who shall enter the portal of the *arcanum* to find the reward which his daring and defiance of prejudice deserve.

'In a word, my project means the examination of the grave of Shakespeare, with the object of searching for evidence to identify the true author of the Plays.

'There are many reasons why I am resolved on this. First and foremost, the grave is the the only authenticated place of Shakespearian associations which remains unsearched. It has not been touched, because the time has not yet arrived for an investigation. Prejudice has preserved the grave; but no one objects when the tomb of a Pharaoh is rifled, and the British, or some other, Museum receives the mummy with scientific joy. Time, as I said before, makes all the difference. I do not propose to go as far as this; for, if there be a body, or the remains of one, even in the condition of dust, I would treat it with infinite respect. My object is not sacrilegious, but a scientific desire to settle a vexed question.

'Another cause for the postponement of this search has undoubtedly been the "terrible curse" put upon him who should undertake it. You remember the doggerel lines, which convey but the one design, that during the last two hundred and seventy years, or thereabouts, have served their purpose.

> ' " Good friend, for Jesus' sake, forbeare
> To digge the dust enclosed here ;
> Bleste be the man that spares thes stones,
> And curst be he that moves my bones."

'What do these commonplace rhymes mean? They have been explained to signify Shakespeare's repugnance to have his bones transferred to the charnel house near the church. This is an explanation as weak as it is absurd. Would the noble-minded Shakespeare, as revealed in his works, care a straw what became of his bones? Do they signify the expression of the wish of a vulgar-minded man to get his bones back on the day of resurrection? or were they an injunction to the world at large to refrain from searching his grave, so that the secret it contained should not be revealed until the fitting time had arrived?

'I think it reasonable to conjecture that the grave contains something more than bones and dust. In addition to the real meaning of the lines on the sepulchre, there is also the fact that the grave was made at the unusual and unnecessary depth of seventeen feet below the surface. Thus to the moral injunction was conjoined the physical difficulty of reaching the grave.

'There is an evident intention to hide something until a period of time shall have elapsed, perhaps until the danger of publishing the name of the true author shall have passed away, or (for some occult reason in the author's mind) until the curiosity, the controversial spirit and the energy of men shall have been aroused to take action. Perhaps the mystery has been due to vanity or pride, or may be the author is laughing at us, and has clothed a most unworthy lay figure with his own splendid garments in derision of our stupidity.

'You will probably ask, If during this long period any documentary evidence were placed in the grave, has it not disappeared by decay, and is it not now so much dust? I have thought of that, and it is probable that some means were adopted to preserve it, such as enclosing it in a metal box, or air-tight case. The individual who took such pains to conceal his identity would be equally careful to preserve its verification.

'Has any attempt ever been made to reach the grave, either by accident or design? Halliwell Phillipps mentions: "The nearest approach to an excavation into the grave of Shakespeare was made in the summer of the year 1796 in digging a vault in the immediate locality, when an opening appeared, which was presumed to indicate the commencement of the site of the bard's remains. The most scrupulous care, however, was taken not to disturb the neighbouring earth in the slightest degree, a clerk having been placed there until the brickwork of the adjoining vault was completed, to prevent anyone from making an examination. No relics whatever were visible through the small opening that thus presented itself; and as the Poet was buried in the ground, not in a vault, the chancel earth, moreover, formerly absorbing a large degree of moisture, the great probability is that dust alone remains." Further on he writes: "It is not many years since a phalanx of trouble-tombs, lanterns and spades in hand, assembled in the chancel at dead of night, intent on disobeying the solemn injunction that the bones of Shakespeare were not to be disturbed. But the supplicatory lines prevailed. There were some among the number who, at the last moment, refused to incur the warning condemnation, and so the design was happily abandoned."

'No! the time had not arrived: they were nearly a hundred years too soon. The world was neither prepared nor ready for the revelation.

'There have been various phases of the Shakespeare cult. First, in the end of the sixteenth and the beginning of the seventeenth centuries, the production of the Plays, either on the stage or in book form, with the Poems, drew admiration from the small minority of the educated classes, to be followed by more or less earnest study and appreciation in the years which ensued. Then occurred a period of stagnation or indifference, to be succeeded by an awakening to the beauty and power of the works as education became more general, until the controversial period arrived, when the problem of the true authorship was presented for solution, and conscientious minds could no longer rest contented with the suspicious and doubtful claim of William Shakespeare, the ignorant butcher of Stratford. His greatest supporters, his most faithful biographers, have been obliged to admit that a man so uneducated as he was must have written the works by an effort of intuitive genius; or, in other words, he was the medium for a miracle, his writing a departure from the usual and natural process of imparting wisdom from acquired knowledge.

'It could only have been by a miracle that he raised, without a foundation, that glorious superstructure, the materials of which are found in the histories and plays of many nations, the stories and legends of Greek and Latin authors, and the romances of the Middle Ages, while he had not read any of them.

'Whether or not the time has arrived for determining the matter remains to be seen. It may be that this advanced age is ripe for the discovery. It may be that we are the selected discoverers. At anyrate, there does not seem to be another unexplored source of information than the grave, and to that I propose we direct our immediate attention.

'I have not been idle in this matter, and, while here, I have made a careful examination of the locality.

'In the early mornings, while you have all been sleeping, I frequently visited the spot and made several careful measurements without being observed, and I declare the project feasible under certain conditions. With the means and time at our disposal, the difficulties and they are not few—may be overcome. It is for you to say whether you will aid in overcoming those difficulties, physical in one sense, and certainly moral in another.'

There was silence for some time after the termination of Geoffrey's fervent appeal. The suggestion was so astounding, so bold, and so disregardful of custom and conventionality, that each waited for the other to answer him, until at last, Doris, with eyes full of enthusiasm said, placing her hand affectionately on his shoulder, 'Where thou goest, I will go!'

'Bravely said,' exclaimed Mr Layton; 'and where you two go, I suppose I must go, so as at least to give you my counsel and advice, should any unusual peril threaten. But what says our friend Richmond?'

'I am entirely with you,' he replied. 'I will sink or swim with you. We are all in the same boat; and whether we arrive safely in port, or sink by the way, I will not desert the ship.'

CHAPTER XVI

THE die was cast. They had embarked on an enterprise which was certainly perilous, and of which they could not forsee the end. Full of ardour, yet cautious to avoid suspicion, they moved with deliberation, and discussed many methods of procedure. Should they effect their purpose by the power of money? Every man has his price. A bribe sufficiently large might be useful, and they might effect in a night that which otherwise would take weeks to obtain. But whom should they bribe? The parish grave-digger, or the parish priest? This idea was dismissed. It would not do to take anyone into their confidence. Finally Geoffrey's plan was decided to be the most feasible, and it was this.

If it were possible to purchase a piece of land, not too far from the church, and drive a tunnel from it in the direction of the chancel, so as to reach the grave, the object of their enterprise would be accomplished; but, was it possible? Was the land to be obtained, and in the right spot? and if so, how could suspicion of their intentions be avoided? Could the tunnel be made by the three men? What was to be done with the earth they were to remove from the excavation? and by what means could they cover up their work after it was done?

The first thing to do was to find the available spot for their operations.

Geoffrey had already provided himself with the largest sized Ordnance Map of Stratford, and he marked on it several positions suitable to the scheme. He made inquiries, but found that nothing was for sale. He and Doris indulged in the pleasurable excitement of house hunting; and although they were easy to please, they discovered none for sale to suit their purpose.

But the power of money will tell. There was a house, with a garden of perhaps a quarter of an acre in extent, which seemed to Geoffrey to be admirably suited. It was within the radius of their intended operations. It was detached, and although inconvenient as a residence, it admitted of additions being made of more rooms and further accommodation. Above all, the area of the property was sufficient for future possibilities. All this he ascertained by calling on the owner, to whom he disclosed his desire to buy. He made no secret of his forthcoming marriage to the lady who accompanied him, and of his intention to purchase for her a residence at Stratford, as near as may be to where her beloved Shakespeare was laid to rest. As he was rich, he was prepared to pay a high price to gratify her whim. The bait took. Geoffrey became the buyer of the property at double its value. The owner regarding Geoffrey as a more than usually eccentric American, whose admiration of the Poet, shared by all his countrymen, was accentuated by his desire to please the lady he was about to marry.

Thus the first practical step was taken.

When possession was given them, arrangements were made with a local architect to make designs for the improvement of the house to render it a suitable residence for the four people who intended to reside there. On the plea of lighting the house electrically, a large wooden shed was put up in the garden, ostensibly as an engine and dynamo house, but with the intention of using it to cover the tunnelling operations, and to conceal the earth they proposed to extract.

It was necessary for Geoffrey to make frequent journeys to London and other places to purchase the tools and other requisites, such as the boring machinery, which was conveyed to the premises in separate pieces, and the motor; an oil engine, which as it was to drive the dynamo for lighting the house, excited no suspicion. Matters were thus pretty well advanced, and Mr Layton, with his daughter, had returned to Fleckton, leaving Geoffrey and Sir Henry in charge, when the latter received a telegram from Chamberlain, the London detective, as follows :—

'Have found our man. Come at once.'

Loth though he was to leave his friends, Sir Henry decided to run up to London, especially as Geoffrey insisted upon it, and pursue the investigation, the success of which meant so much for his happiness.

CHAPTER XVII

ARRIVED in town, he met the detective by appointment, and learnt from that intelligent person that he was on the track of the suspected object of their search.

'You must know, Sir Henry,' said he, 'that, having very few facts to work on, I have had to invent theories and follow them up. The ordinary channels of inquiry yielded no results. I became very friendly with the servants in the family town house, and made more than one journey to the places in the country to obtain a clue, but with barren results. I only found that my man had been cast off by his relatives as a reprobate, and that his address was unknown. This suggested that, if alive, he must have assumed another name and another appearance. He might have left the country for a more congenial Continental gambling haunt, where his talent for manipulating cards would provide him a living as a *chevalier d'industrie*. Then I considered it would be better to exhaust the inquiry in London before attempting a search abroad. I believed, from the character I had heard of him, he would resort to no honest work, and I visited most of the shady places in town where gambling was carried on. I sauntered into billiard rooms, I attended race meetings, and I was introduced into many second and third class clubs—some of which have honoured me by membership. I made many acquaintances, and more than once I thought I had spotted some one like the man I was after; but he would not fit in with my theory of him. Either his age was in error — for Burke's *Peerage* had given me that—or he had not the unmistakable air of broken-down swelldom which is so hard to shake off; or he was not sufficiently skilful in his card playing; for I flatter myself I know pretty well every dodge and trick to which a cardsharper resorts.

'I had pictured him in my mind as a dissipated-looking man, pale and thin, with the long fingers of a trickster of cards, with some remnant of good breeding left in him: but you will see for yourself how much I was mistaken.

'I will take you to a club to-night where you will meet with a man of quite the opposite appearance—hale, bluff and countrified, with a demeanour of honesty about him, except in his eyes, which he cannot disguise. Yet I have reason to believe him to be our man, simply because I have found him out in being the most accomplished manipulator of cards I ever saw. His style is absolutely perfect. His methods are mostly original and unexpected; but he is wasting his talent where he is at present—although he may have some object in view—perhaps waiting for a grand coup, after which he will clear out.

'We will give him the opportunity if you like. My plan is this: Although you were members of the same club, yet you have never met each other, because he was elected while you were on your travels, and when you returned he had left the club. Therefore he will have no fear you will recognise him. He knows of you, there is no doubt, and is aware of the fact of your wealth. It is more than likely he will regard you as a possible pigeon to be plucked. I will take you to the club and introduce you to the card table. By-the-bye, what games of cards do you know?'

'Since my college days,' replied Sir Henry, 'I have played but little. I know something of whist and piquet.'

'Your knowledge is of no use for the present purpose. Do you know baccarat or écarté?'

'A little of the latter and nothing of the former.'

'Well, we must improve your knowledge of écarté, for that is the game that will give us our opportunity with him. It is not necessary for you to be a master of the game; in fact, a little knowledge in this instance will be the useful thing; you will be the easier victim. I will arrange you shall play with him. You will find yourself a winner in the beginning. The stakes will be increased. He will most likely let you win a few hundreds. The lookers on will be betting—backing you or your opponent—for you must remember they do not know his real character or your motives. Presently you will find that a run of luck in his favour will set in and you will begin to lose.

You must keep your head, if you can, so as not to awake his suspicions. Do not refuse to increase the stakes, and this is what will happen.' So saying, Chamberlain produced from his pocket a pack of cards, and proceeded to play several games of écarté with Sir Henry, explaining, as he went on, the nice points of the game, and showing him not only the commonplace cardsharper's trick of producing the useful and necessary king, but also the more artistic methods of the dealer in placing any cards he chooses into his own and his opponent's hands.

Chamberlain further explained: 'The man we hope to meet to-night is doubtless prepared for any emergency. I have no doubt he has a store of kings and other cards about him of the same pattern as those in use at the club, with mechanical means of producing them at will; and I intend, at the critical moment, when you have lost a few thousands—on paper, for no money or cheques need pass—to accuse our man of cheating. There will be a row. He, of course, will be highly indignant. He may show fight; but before he will have time for any active defence I will get hold of him, and as I know exactly where he keeps his concealed cards and apparatus, there will be no difficulty in dragging them forth as proofs of my accusation. Even the members of the Pandemonium Club will be astonished—for, to give them their due, they draw the line at card cheating, especially when it is found out. We shall have them all with us, and then—'

'And then,' said Sir Henry, 'it appears to me, we shall have exposed a cheat; but that is all. I fail to see the connection between him and the man who caused the ruin of my friend Rupert Ellerslie.'

'I see it is necessary for me to tell you everything,' replied Chamberlain, 'and I think you will find I have absolute proof they are the same. When I first discovered him, and was led to make further investigation because of his ability as a cardsharper, I had him shadowed and carefully watched. It was not long before the knowledge of his living-place was obtained —a room in a mean street on the south side of the Thames—and it was not long before, under an ordinary pretext, I made an examination of his apartment, in the owner's absence. I took the liberty of picking the lock of a small writing-case on his dressing table, and found therein letters from his noble father and other members of his family; and, to do them justice, they have worked hard to reclaim him before casting him off. Some notes and memoranda in his own handwriting, which I had no difficulty in comparing and identifying with his writing at the Pandemonium Club, a signet ring with the family crest, and, in fact, evidence enough in the writing-case, and in the room itself, to satisfy the most doubting mind.'

'This is indeed good news,' said the delighted Sir Henry. 'I congratulate myself upon having asked your assistance. And how about the future? What do you propose to do?'

'Well,' replied Chamberlain, 'having unmasked our man, and having proved to ourselves and to others his true character, we will then follow him up, and I shall be surprised if you and I together do not obtain a confession from him. He will be very much down on his luck, and broken in spirit. This class of man might be induced to speak the truth for a consideration, and a visit to him may yield good and, perhaps, unexpected results. But the time has come for you to dine and dress. I will call for you at ten o'clock. Remember, please, that I am Mr Fortescue; but there is no necessity for you to disguise your name or appearance.'

CHAPTER XVIII

AT ten o'clock Chamberlain presented himself at Sir Henry's hotel, and sent up his card as Mr Fortescue. He was not only faultlessly attired in evening dress, but had taken other means of sinking the detective into the man about town.

When they drove away together in a hansom Sir Henry complimented him upon his transformation.

The Pandemonium Club, to those who know it, is, so far as regards locality and class, just on the borders of Clubland. It is a proprietary establishment of mushroom growth, which imitates the Pall Mall article in many ways; but, like most establishments of the same kind, is an unlicensed tavern, if anything. Membership is not so difficult to secure as in the Athenæum, but then to be blackballed there is no disgrace, whereas, to be served in the same manner at the Pandemonium is a stigma indeed. One must be an out and out bad character to be ineligible for the Pandemonium. The features of the club are bad wines, pretentious and expensive food, billiards and baccarat, poker and écarté. Among the members are more betting men than bishops, and the odds about any event, racing and otherwise, can be obtained at any hour of the day and night—especially the night. The club keeps its doors open while any two of its members remain playing cards—for fines after one o'clock are the chief source of income to the proprietor.

Sir Henry and Fortescue soon found themselves in the smoking-room, which was the rendezvous of members before gambling commenced. They smoked their cigars and drank their whiskies, and looked about them. Fortescue informed Sir Henry that their man had not yet arrived. 'He calls himself James Salter; and, if he comes into the room to-night, I wonder if you will recognise him from my description. I think it will be well we should get into conversation with some of those who are present. I will, when the occasion arrives, introduce you to one or two, so as to pave the way for him when he comes.'

A break in the conversation permitted Fortescue to interject a remark which led, naturally, to the mentioning of his friend's name, and it was observable, by the deference paid him, that the club felt itself honoured by the presence of Sir Henry Richmond—a man of title and wealth—two distinctions unusual in members of, and visitors to, the Pandemonium. The utmost friendliness was shown him, and conversation was at its height when James Salter entered.

Sir Henry gave Fortescue an expressive look, which was answered by a slight movement of the detective's eyelid, and soon after Salter joined the circle and supplied his quota to the intelligent, if not intellectual, general remarks.

When half-an-hour had thus passed some one suggested an adjournment to the card room upstairs, and a move was made there.

Sir Henry and Fortescue were soon seated at a whist table with two others, who expressed themselves afterwards that 'The baronet was a very agreeable fellow, but that he could not play whist a little bit,' which was perfectly true, for his knowledge of whist was derived from the few games he had played in his college days. Several brilliant displays of wrong play evinced his originality. He showed himself to be quite a learned doctor in the ethics of the 'play of the involuntary card,' until his partner nearly had a fit in restraining himself from swearing. Then, when the rubber ended, the table broke up, and the poker room was visited, where a party of five were enjoying a pleasant gamble of two pounds limit.

Salter, who had followed Sir Henry from the whist room, where he had been an observer of his play, sat down by his side, stood drinks to those about him, and made himself generally agreeable.

But why prolong a description of the double plot which was in progress? When the two chief actors were only too desirous of bringing about its success, the result was assured, and it happened pretty well on the same lines as the detective had predicted.

At about one o'clock in the morning all the members then in the club had assembled round the card table at which Sir Henry and Salter were playing écarté, attracted there by the high play. All other amusements had been given up. The poker tables were deserted, the billiard room gave up its contents, and everyone was more or less excited at looking on at a game where hundreds of pounds might be won or lost at the turn of a card.

The stakes had been doubled more than once. Sir Henry was a loser of some thousands. The lookers-on were breathless with excitement. Then the moment arrived when Chamberlain concluded it was time to act. He suddenly seized Salter's hand and, with a wrench, turned it up and disclosed a king in its palm. Salter jumped up. Chamberlain made a dash at his chest, tore up his waistcoat, and before Salter could do or say anything in self-defence, the detective dragged forth a curious contrivance of springs and wires, with a holdfast to which was attached several cards. He had not done with him, for as Salter, with a howl of rage, drove his fist into the detective's face—a blow which the latter neatly avoided—Chamberlain tripped him up so that he fell, and before he had time to rise he found himself pinioned with the left arm of his assailant, while more cards were being produced from his pockets.

Then he was allowed to get up from the ground. He glared around him. He saw no sympathy in the faces of the excited crowd. This was no time for defence. What could he say or do? He had been caught in the act, and the game was up. He slunk towards the door, the members making way for him. He made a rush for the stairs. Amid shouts of derision and resentment he gained the street, and disappeared for ever from the Pandemonium Club.

CHAPTER XIX

ON the day following the episode at the club Sir Henry and Chamberlain met to decide upon the next step. They came to the conclusion to strike at once. So the detective proposed to his companion to provide himself with a couple of thousand pounds in bank notes for possible emergencies, and then they took a cab and drove across the river to Salter's lodgings.

The cab was discharged at the corner of the street, and they walked to the house and rang the bell. The door was opened by a slatternly woman who, on their inquiring for Mr Salter, and saying they were friends of his, directed them to the second floor front, at the door of which they knocked and then walked in.

Salter was lying on his bed half dressed, with a pipe in his mouth.

He sprang up on seeing his visitors, and, with a look of fear and surprise on his face, said, 'What the devil do you want?'

'A few minutes' talk with you, Mr Salter,' replied Chamberlain.

'And what if I refuse to have anything to do with you?'

'Then you will have to listen whether you like it or not,' said Chamberlain, as he walked to the door, locked it, and put the key in his pocket.

'Sir Henry Richmond and I,' he continued, 'are here to make amends of a certain kind for the unpleasant scene of last night, and to purchase of you some information.'

'Oh! you have come to apologise.'

'No! not to apologise,' said Sir Henry, 'hardly that; but as our little game of cards was the cause of the inevitable disaster to your present prospects, I am anxious to make you a substantial recompense.'

'That's very good of you,' said Salter; 'but this generosity means something more. Out with it.'

'It does mean something more; and, with your permission, we will sit down.'

'By all means,' sneered Salter. 'I am sorry I can offer you no refreshment.'

'Thanks, it is not necessary; but if you will give me your attention I think it will be sufficient.'

'Go ahead,' replied Salter.

'Well then,' said Sir Henry, 'I will commence by asking a question. Would you be surprised to hear that our little game of écarté was got up especially for your benefit?'

'What the devil do you mean? A plant?'

'Yes,' remarked Chamberlain, 'a plant, and an entirely successful one. I arranged it.'

'You!' said the enraged Salter. 'Damn you! Fortescue; what for? Of all the fellows at the Pandemonium I never thought you were on the cross.'

'Perhaps it will clear matters a little if I tell you my name is not Fortescue.'

'There's nothing new in that: there are several Howards, Montagues and Cecils at the club.'

'Yes;' replied Chamberlain, 'I am not the only one there who has assumed a name with an object. My name is Chamberlain, and I am a detective. But perhaps Sir Henry had better go on now.'

With a glance at the locked door and the window, the hunted man, ashy pale from rage and fear, retired to his seat on the bed. He ground his teeth with rage, opened and closed his fists and growled, 'You have trapped me I can't help listening to you. Go on.'

'Yes,' said Sir Henry, 'I frankly tell you it was necessary to unmask you to succeed in the object I have in view. For I know you. I know who you are, and that Salter is not your true name. You have assumed it instead of your family one.'

'I deny it,' shouted Salter.

'Perhaps,' said Chamberlain, quietly, as he tapped with his stick the writing-case on the dressing table, 'this box contains some information on the subject. Go on, Sir Henry.'

'Devil!' hissed the cowed Salter as he sank on his seat.

'About four years ago you were a member of a West End club, to which also belonged a friend of mine, Rupert Ellerslie, and at the baccarat table one night, when he and you were present, an accusation of card cheating was made, and he, though innocent, had to suffer for the wrongdoing of someone else. I want to prove his innocence. Can you assist me?'

'I know nothing about it,' sullenly replied Salter.

'Come, come, my friend,' said Chamberlain; 'you surely remember it?'

'I know nothing about it, I tell you.'

'Will anything make you remember it? Say, for example, a liberal present in ready money. How much?'

'To remember it?' said Salter, with a gleam of cunning in his eye. 'A thousand!'

'We are getting on nicely,' said Chamberlain; and how much to clear Mr Ellerslie?'

'Ten thousand.'

'No business to be done to-day, I see,' said Chamberlain. 'You estimate the value of your services at too high a figure. Besides, I ought to tell you that we only want your assistance to complete the transaction. With Sir Henry's and my evidence of the disclosure of last night, and this little packet of documents, which you recognise as having been abstracted from the writing-case on the dressing table, we have a fairly strong case, which, doubtless, you will consider a negative one. I admit it; and as I always, or nearly always, play with my cards on the table— Do not wince Salter. I did not mean to hurt your feelings. Sir Henry is willing to pay for your help. What do you think of a couple of thou.? Think of the possibilities such a sum discloses for you- in South Africa or Australia. With your talent, you can soon turn it into the ten thousand you jokingly mentioned.'

'Make it five.'

'I regret I am unable to advise Sir Henry to make it more than two. Besides, that is the exact sum he has with him. It is after banking hours; and if it were not, we do not care to leave you to get more.'

'What do you want me to do?'

'To write a confession of the truth.'

And then Sir Henry went over his pocket-book, from which he took the bank notes and laid them on the table. Salter moved from off the bed to the dressing table, opened the writing-case, extracted a sheet of paper, pen and ink, walked back to the table, laid the sheet by the side of the notes and wrote some lines, which he signed in his true name. He handed the document to Sir Henry, who read it, and passed it on to the detective, who remarked, 'Yes, that will do.' Both he and Sir Henry attached their names as witnesses. The bank notes were given to Salter, with the papers belonging to him, and with a quiet 'good afternoon' all round, the two took their departure.

CHAPTER XX

Sir Henry permitted but little time to elapse before he had effectually cleared the character of Rupert from the stigma cast upon it. The committee of his club were glad to reinstate him. The production of the confession, signed by the true delinquent and witnessed by Richmond and Chamberlain, was at once accepted as ample vindication of Ellerslie's innocence. There was a unanimous feeling that immediate steps should be taken to bring him back from his self-imposed exile. The most distinguished personage in the club graciously volunteered to write him an autograph letter, expressing his particular opinion of him, congratulating him upon the complete exoneration of his character and inviting him to return.

Sir Henry received the letter to be forwarded to Ellerslie, together with special permission to show it previously to Rupert's father, mother, sister and friends, and as it contained a particular paragraph indicating the writer's opinion that he was never one of those who believed in Rupert's guilt, it was an unusually valuable and reassuring testimonial. Sir Henry sent a telegram to the family at Ellerslie Court announcing the joyful news, and followed it up with letters to them and to his friends at Stratford. He then found the names of the best known firm of lawyers in Toronto, and telegraphed them to spare no time, effort or money in communicating with Rupert at the Great Manitoulin Island, or wherever he might be, and to tell him the good news. As the search was an easy one—for Rupert was found without much difficulty under such *carte blanche* instructions—Sir Henry's cup of joy was filled to the brim. A telegram was received, both by him and the Ellerslies, telling them of Rupert's intention to return at once, and Sir Henry timed his visit to Ellerslie Court (to which he had been earnestly invited) so as to be present at the moment of Rupert's happy arrival at the home of his delighted parents. Words cannot describe the meeting—the joy of the Ellerslies and their thankfulness to Sir Henry.

What more fitting occasion could there be for Sir Henry to declare his love to Linda? None, surely; and accordingly one morning he told the gentle maiden of his love, and shyly but consciously she permitted her heart to speak her responsive feelings.

This happy result was regarded by Mr and Mrs Ellerslie and Rupert as a fitting and most delightful sequence to Sir Henry's achievement, for which, indeed, they felt unending gratitude; and how could they better prove it than by welcoming him into their family as a beloved member of it.

No one was more pleased than Lady Richmond to hear of her son's choice. Sir Henry took Linda over to Fleckton, accompanied by her mother, father and Rupert, and universal joy reigned.

All this time our friends at Stratford were constantly engaged in the great enterprise. Geoffrey, who had been left in charge, had, assisted by Mr Layton and Doris, furnished the reconstructed cottage. The shed had been built in the garden and fitted with the engine to drive the dynamo for the electric light, and for the more important purpose of working the boring machinery. The trio moved into the cottage, and a letter was despatched to Sir Henry informing him they only waited for his arrival to begin the work, and he, loth as he was to leave his lady love, responded loyally, and soon arrived on the scene of action.

CHAPTER XXI

DIARY OF GEOFFREY

I HAVE put in the form of a diary the events which follow our acquisition of the cottage and garden.

Our establishment comprises an elderly female as cook and two maids, chosen for their sedate, not to say stupid, appearance, presided over by my bright and beautiful Doris; but as appearances are deceitful, our obtuse-looking servants are warned, as an additional precaution, not to enter or even to go near the shed in the garden, which, whether we are in or out of it, is always kept locked. Besides, I think my short lecture to them on the dangers of electricity in general, and of our installation in particular, with the additional terror of the oil engine, will effectually extinguish any curiosity they may feel to make a surreptitious visit to the place where our secret operations will be carried on.

The shed is a spacious building, lighted only from the glazed roof, and with no windows at the sides. A small lean-to at one end contains the electric accumulators. Inside the shed is an oil engine of sufficient power to drive the dynamo, as well as to supply the necessary energy to drive boring tools, and to work a hoist and other machinery, all of which I purchased in London, Birmingham and elsewhere, and have had brought here at various times and in separate pieces. My knowledge of mechanics has enabled me, with the assistance of Mr Layton, to put everything in place after the engine and dynamo had been set up by workmen from London. We have also a pump, worked by the engine, if it be found necessary to extract water from the pit, which we intend to sink at least eighteen and a half feet down, and from nearly the bottom of which we intend to drive an adit passage towards the chancel of the church. This adit is to be on a slightly upward incline, so that we shall have a dry path

to work on. The object of our search
is supposed to be seventeen feet below the
surface; but whether the bottom or the top
of the grave is that distance down is impossible to say, or whether, indeed, the state
ment is altogether incorrect or not remains
to be seen. I have carefully taken the
compass bearings, and have measured on the
ordnance map the exact distance. Our
tunnel will be driven through comparatively
easy soil; but if we meet with obstacles, we
must perforce overcome them—for we have
time, energy and the means to do so.
We propose to light the tunnel electrically,
and to fit it with bell communication to
the house, so that warning may be given
us of danger from intrusive visitors. Our
plans are to work only a few hours every
day, not only to render our labour easier,
but by frequently showing ourselves out
walking, riding and driving, to avert any
suspicion. Everything necessary has, I believe,
been provided. The shed, our workshop,
is, to my mind, as complete for our purpose
as forethought can make it. The easy-
running engine and dynamo, the lathe and

the rest of the machinery and tools, give a serious aspect to the scene. They remind me of the arduous labour we have taken upon ourselves and the responsibilities of the undertaking, and it is without any misgiving or self-reproach that I wonder what its termination will be.

November 1st, 1894.—Henry Richmond arrived and received, with great satisfaction, our congratulations on his happy engagement to Linda Ellerslie. The sympathetic tie which unites us gains strength by his new happiness, in which we all partake. No one was more sincere in her good wishes than my dear Doris, who had already expressed to me her expectations and hopes that the loves of Linda and Henry might be fittingly realised.

In the afternoon I showed him over the workshop, of which he expressed his great admiration. The only doubt he seemed to have was that the labour of shaft sinking and tunnel driving would be too much for the three of us, and that we might require help. I replied that what we wanted in strength we could make up by taking time, and that I saw no necessity for admitting anyone to our secrets. He suggested that, if extra aid were absolutely necessary, his future brother-in-law, Rupert, an athletic young fellow and thoroughly devoted to him, might be called in.

November 3d.—We started work. A ring, four feet six inches in diameter, was marked on the ground at a spot we selected as a good position for the shaft, and my dear Doris was invited to take the first spadeful of earth from the surface we broke up for the purpose. We had donned our working clothes, and made very respectable navvies. Richmond and I, with pickaxe and shovel, made fair progress, while Mr Layton helped in removing the earth to the large unoccupied space in the shed reserved for the purpose. I had calculated that if it were insufficient we could form new flower beds out in the garden with the surplus without suspicion. We worked for two hours, and then broke off.

During the next six days we worked for two or three hours each day.

November 10th.—We rigged up our

derrick and connected it to the engine; for we had got down deep enough to require mechanical aid in lifting the baskets of earth from the shaft, and by means of an inclined plane and a tipping arrangement the soil was more easily conveyed away.

November 11th.—This day arrived Lady Richmond, Mr and Mrs Ellerslie, Linda and Rupert. This visit had become absolutely necessary; for, in spite of daily letters to and fro between Henry and Linda, he had so longed to see his sweetheart that I feared he might break loose and rush off to the Court to her. So Mr Layton and I, in secret council, decided to recommend that they should be asked to come to us for a few days. They put up at the hotel. We gave ourselves a holiday, which was devoted to our friends. Mr Layton waited upon Lady Richmond. We engaged couples found ourselves sufficiently interested, and the only one out in the cold was the stalwart Rupert, whose muscular appearance we viewed with admiration, not altogether disconnected with its utility in a certain laborious work we had in hand. He behaved very well, and together with Mr Ellerslie, took great interest in all the Shakespearian objects in and about the town, and evinced no curiosity, whatever he may have felt, in the secluding of ourselves in Stratford. Remembering that the day might come when we should be obliged to ask for Rupert's aid, I thought that it would perhaps be wise to give him a present hint of our purpose; but, on second thoughts, I considered it better to refrain. The dangerous quest in which we are engaged, with many doubts of what the future has in store, requires extreme caution in imparting our secret, and in binding the conscience of anyone who may not possess sufficient enthusiasm to make the process easy.

November 14*th.*—Our friends have gone, and Richmond is himself again. We resume work with increased activity, and make considerable progress with our shaft sinking. We expected to find trouble from water, and are prepared with the necessary pumping apparatus, but are agreeably surprised at the dryness of the soil as we descend. This is to be accounted for by the absence of rain during the season, and the natural porosity of the ground we are working in.

November 15th to the 20th.—The sinking proceeded without other incident than the breaking down of the hoist on the last day, which necessitated a visit to Birmingham to purchase new pulleys and ropes.

November 24th.—While at work down below, the danger signal, sounding twice, denoted visitors to the cottage. I ascended the ladder. We resumed our every-day clothes and sauntered into the house. We had visitors indeed. A carriage-load of distinguished county people and friends of the Richmonds were in our small drawing-room. They had heard of Lady Richmond's visit to Stratford, and of Sir Henry living there. They had called, probably out of curiosity, and certainly for social reasons, and we had some difficulty in explaining away our selection of Stratford as a home. The air was full of danger; but our visitors, much to our relief, were too polite to press us further, and they left with the impression that we were afflicted with an American form of Shakespearian lunacy.

Hitherto we had not been troubled with

visitors. The parson had called, as a matter of duty to the newcomers into his parish. When he left, we compared notes and found we had each been thinking of the same thing—what his feelings would be if he knew the object of our choice of Stratford as an abiding-place? Outwardly calm, but inwardly quaking with terror, we had passed that *mauvais quart d'heure*, and sincerely hoped he would never repeat his visit.

November 30th. — By this date we had finished the shaft, the base of which we enlarged considerably, so as to admit of the simple machinery for driving the tunnel, which we placed in position without delay.

December 3d.—Began tunnelling, and made fair progress through the soft earth. As the work proceeded we retained the roof with suitable lengths of board, and upheld it with props. We lighted the gallery with incandescent lamps from the dynamo above, and, as a piece of engineering work, we could not but feel satisfied with our labours.

With an occasional breakdown and stoppage for repairs the following days were passed.

We met with stones and portions of ancient tree roots, which required to be extricated by hard manual labour, and their removal and hoisting to the surface were not accomplished easily. Any moisture that percolated through the tunnel flowed to the well we had made at the bottom of the shaft, and was pumped up to the surface through a pipe to a trough into the garden, and our gallery was quite dry.

As the work progressed I could not but feel an increased anxiety regarding the ultimate result. The responsibility of the undertaking, shared in, it is true, by my dear friends with an unexampled cheerfulness and devotion, seemed to me to be entirely my own; for was not I the prime mover in this extraordinary enterprise? Was it not I who had fired their imagination and made them parties to a scheme, the morality of which and its success were at least doubtful? And I say now that, were it not for the encouragement and support of my darling Doris, who in her love for me had identified herself with all my thoughts and read my inmost soul, I might have failed in my purpose.

Whatever my two companions thought—and probably they had the same misgivings as myself—they did not impart them either to each other or to me. It was, therefore, a joyful moment to us all when I announced one day that, according to my calculations, we were nearing the end of our labours, and that within a few hours we should, if no untoward accident happened, strike the grave. We retired to rest that night full of suppressed excitement at the prospect of the revelation which the next day might yield.

CHAPTER XXII

In the morning, after breakfast, we went to work, having arranged with my enthusiastic Doris that we would send to the cottage a signal from the shed to tell her when she should come to us. The engine and machinery were set going. Mr Layton was left on the top to look after matters there while Henry and I descended to our underground work.

According to the compass and my measurements on the map we should be in close proximity to the grave; so we proceeded with our excavation cautiously, and with constant observation for any signs that might indicate the spot we were in search of. We thus proceeded until it seemed to me that only a few inches of earth intervened. I was holding a short, iron tool against the surface, which Henry was in the act of driving in with a hammer. He had delivered a few blows, causing the earth round about the tool to shake. This was indeed an indication of a hollow space beyond, and when suddenly from the other side came a noise— a curious, weird and unexpected metallic sound—we paused and looked at each other.

'What is that?' Henry whispered. We were rivetted to the spot. The most abject terror seized us, and we rushed, as best we could, down the gallery and up the ladder to the surface, where we surprised Mr Layton with our chattering teeth and pale faces. It took us some time to recover ourselves and explain, and here the common sense of our friend Layton assisted us.

'You cannot,' said he, for a moment believe that the sound you heard had any other than a natural cause. It was sufficiently startling, no doubt, and considering the circumstances, you need not be ashamed of your fright. You had, by the blows on the wall caused it to vibrate, and so displaced something on the other side, which, in falling, made the noise. I will go down with you this time and assist.' But this we would not hear of. Henry declared he was better; and we agreed with Mr Layton that it was no supernatural warning or manifestation, but due to a commonplace cause. We rested awhile, and then descended once more.

A description of what followed, when we resumed our labours, reads like a romance, but it is, nevertheless, actually true.

We succeeded in removing a sufficiently large piece of the intervening earth to enable us to discover that on the other side was an open space of irregular formation, and by the light of a lamp we saw, with feelings of reverential awe, that it was indeed a grave, within which lay a decayed, mouldering coffin. The side and a portion of the top had fallen away, disclosing indication of its tenant. Half in and half out of the coffin lay an object, which seemed to have fallen from its original position. It had rounded sides, and was flat at each end. It puzzled us to think what it might be. There was nothing else in sight; simply the bones of the dead Shakespeare, which we, in obedience to his wish, took care not to move, and this cylinder. It was within arm's reach; so, stretching forth my hand, I with some difficulty grasped it, and brought it out. It was light in weight, and when we rubbed off the incrustation we found that it was made of metal. What could it be? What did it contain?

Suddenly, with a cry of joy, I said to Henry, 'Herein is the great secret. This cylinder is the depository of the truth. We have succeeded in our search!'

'Then,' replied Henry, grasping my hand, 'we are rewarded indeed. Let us return at once, consult Layton, and decide on the next step. So, carefully bearing the precious cylinder, we got to the surface, and showed our prize to the anxious Mr Layton.

Then we sent the signal to the cottage, and my darling quickly arrived, full of excitement and hope.

The adventures we had experienced were related, and we concluded that the mysterious sounds we had heard were fully explained by the evident falling of the metal cylinder at the critical moment of our approach.

We held a hurried council, and there was

no dissentient to the proposal to take action at once, and, by opening the mysterious cylinder disclose its secret contents.

We examined it with great care. It was of copper, carefully made and hermetically put together. There was no lid or concealed opening. The whole was smooth and without joint; about ten inches long, and three and a half inches in diameter. Were it not light in weight and hollow in sound, it might have been, to all appearances, a solid body. Whatever it was, and whatever it contained, it was surely intended to preserve, to protect, an article of value. But what? And how should we open it? We considered. It must be done carefully. Several suggestions were made. We weighed it in the scales. It was examined over and over again. Was there any spot thinner or weaker than another, which admitted of an easier entrance? No; it was the same throughout. How should it be done? The lathe? Yes, the lathe would do it. Fitting it, therefore, carefully in between the pivots, I worked the treadle and applied a cutting tool to one of the ends. In a few minutes the work was done; and taking away the cylinder, we gathered around in breathless excitement to see what it might contain.

There was something white inside. I said to Doris. 'You shall draw it forth.'

'No,' she replied, 'it is more fitting that you, who have led us thus far to success, shall be the first discoverer.'

Mr Layton and Henry thought so too, but I refused. 'Let Doris do it,' I said. 'She and I are one in thought. She has shared our anxieties, has bravely encouraged and supported us throughout, and she shall crown the discovery.'

Doris looked at each of us, saw assent in our faces, and without difficulty drew from the cylinder a roll of parchment, which she unwound and handed to me.

There was writing on it. The whole of one side was filled with it, the other was blank.

In the half light of the dying day, amid a silence which denoted almost a suspension of the heart's action, such was the concentration of my listeners' attention, I deciphered and read out the secret the document revealed.

It was written in characters and spelling

of the sixteenth century, in a clear and firm hand, and it read:—

'Not for this age nor for any man alive doe I write this. The Courte and the Countrie are alike steeped in Ignorance and Swinish Practices. I scorn them alle. I use Men for mine own purposes. I move them unknown to themselves: some I raise, who in conceit believe themselves their own Arbiters; some I caste down, catching them in nets they have spread for others; some I lure with Bribes of golde. To them all I am unknowne, or onlie in disguise. I am alone; and with potency more than that of Princes and Rulers of the earth it hath pleased me to moulde the mindes of Men with my secret processes, even by Mind compelling Mind. The Cause is outside the Grand Circle; within it Man hath power. I use it when I neede. I make happier the Fewe that understande. Hereafter more shall joye. I smile at Credulitie, that beleeveth whatsoe'er be spoken. Because I have put my Cloake on to William Shakespeare they say it fitteth him well. Had I chosen a

Goat and turned him loose among them, they were not more fooled. I write this (I say) not for these, but for those who shall, when Centuries roll awaie, with wiser Eyes and Mindes more subtle, demande the Truth. In that Daie I shall be with them (for this I saie—Life is continuous, and as its gross Tenement, with all Things of the Earth, disappeareth not, althoughe they change form). A Generation shall live, of whom some shall have gotten knowledge, and with it slowe cominge Wisdom approaching myne owne, who shall in secret, or following Publick Demande, make the discoverie. The secret worker shall observe restore and retire. The private Waie is fulle of Danger. The Rightfullenesse of an Acte goeth by numbers. It is my Will that those bold enough to dare the deede in secret concerte make it knowne and worke (as I have done privilie) to the end desired. Nay, more, that for mine owne purpose, and that the silent movinge Hand shall not be fitted to its proper Stock until the fulfilment of my designe, I keepe my name unknowne, but not for alwaie. Wisdom is doled out for rewarde to great labour, and fewe there be with merite sufficient to receive and use it; but be Contente, accepte with Thankfulnes and knowe that when it pleaseth the Master Minde further to illume the Intellectes of Men (as that Daie shall come surelie but slowlie) then the Curtaine shall be drawne and the dark backward of Human Historie be plainly seene with that which shall happen in the Future Daies.'

When I had finished no one spoke. The evening shadows had increased, and it almost seemed there had come to us with the document from the grave a spiritual presence to impress us. Doris came closer to my side; Henry and Mr Layton were looking particularly uncomfortable, when the common sense of the latter came to our rescue. He stepped nimbly to the switch board and turned on the electric light. The effect was wonderful. We all plucked up courage and resumed our normal cheerfulness.

It was time to return to the cottage, and we carried our prize with us.

After resting and partaking of a good dinner, the parchment roll was again spread

out and read and re-read. The words
brought to our minds the majestic being
who had written them. His spiritual entity
might be vibrating in our midst at that
moment, watching us and influencing our
thoughts. Who was he? We searched the
scroll again and again for internal evidence
of his identity, but without success; neither
was there figure in history which answered
to his personality. His indomitable indifference to the appreciation or the recognition
of his fellow creatures had closed the door
to inquiry. His was the policy of silence
and to do great deeds, with no desire for
fame. There was one thing clear—his contemptuous reference to William Shakespeare,
and his sneer at the people who believed
him to be the author of the works written
by another. And who can doubt that the
great unknown who wrote the parchment
scroll claims the authorship for himself?
Because I have put my 'cloake on William
Shakespeare they think it fits him well.'
These words are explicit; and if we have not
included in our discovery the name of the
true author, we have at least found that

Shakespeare was not he. Shakespeare was but the medium through whom worked another, greater than he and all men besides. Shakespeare has been sufficiently honoured by the selection of himself by this mental demigod as the vehicle, and has thus derived a surreptitious celebrity too long a time for the patience of man to tolerate.

At least we moderns have for some time not thought the 'cloake fits him well.'

Have my companions and I been chosen by the same great master to work out the solution of the problem? Are we but instruments directed by him to the end we have reached? It looks like it; and when I remember what has passed, how that every circumstance of our meeting, and every event of our lives while together, have been conducive to a predestined and ultimate object, I am more than ever convinced there has been and is guidance and method in the process. I perceive, also, that in addition to our satisfaction as successful discoverers, there has been intermingled with the search from first to last so much happiness to ourselves and to those near and dear to us, that I must conclude there has been purpose and intention manifested throughout. We all see this, and our joy and gratitude are great indeed.

At least, we can show our obligation by attending implicitly to the directions of the great unknown Author by restoring the parchment scroll to the grave, and by this act of restitution show our obedience to his will. Dare we, in all humility, place with it in the copper cylinder a record of our own, an announcement of our discovery or not? It is decided not to do so, but, while imitating the great master, although for an opposite reason, in remaining unknown and unidentified, we shall yet carry out his directions and, with fictitious names, publish to the world an account of our discovery, with every event of our lives during the progress of our search set forth to show their connection with it, the shaping of the end, and our own great happiness.

CHAPTER XXIII

THE next morning we made a careful transcript of the document, and Henry, who had some knowledge of photography, borrowed a camera and took several negatives of it and the cylinder. I went into the town and found a tinman's shop, the proprietor of which sold me the materials and tools for soldering metal, giving me a few lessons into the bargain. I returned to the cottage, and we adjourned to the workshop. We took a last look at the scroll, wondering to ourselves when it would see the light again; then we rolled it up, and Doris, at my request, placed it into the cylinder, to which I soldered the top, making at least an air-tight job of it, if it were not quite so neat as it might have been; but this was my first attempt in that line—probably I shall never be required to undertake another.

Henry and I then descended the shaft. The light was turned on, and we walked up the gallery. Everything was as when we had left it the day before. I passed my hand through the orifice and deposited the cylinder by the side of what remained of the bones of Shakespeare for the next comer, whoever he might be. We took a last lingering look at the scene. I felt triumphant at our success, and thankful that it had been accomplished without accident. If we could not give to the world the name of the great author, his purpose had thus far been carried out by us, and we would persevere to the end he indicates. The glorious crown, which for so long a time had been worn by the Usurper, should be apportioned by our aid to its rightful possessor, that all men might know the truth, and believe, if they chose to do so.

With this resolve we closed the orifice and commenced the labour of refilling that end of the gallery with earth, a work by no means an easy one to perform, remembering that as the tunnel was on an incline the task was an arduous one to bring the earth uphill. No doubt this encumbrance gave rise to the proposal to leave it in its then state, first removing the supporting boards from the ceiling and sides and the props and beams which we had inserted. Time would do the rest and it would fall in.

Day after day we worked at refilling the shaft, in which, or in the tunnel, we left the boring machinery and excavating tools, our shovels, pickaxes, baskets, and other articles for which we now had no use and which would be troublesome to dispose of.

At last we had finished our labour. The surface was restored to its former condition, the floor of the shed was put back, and every trace of our mining work was obliterated or removed. We decided to retain the property in our own possession for ever, so as to avoid the possibility of another owner or tenant finding traces of our designs. It was left in charge of a respectable widow and her daughter as caretakers, whose duties, encouraged by a liberal weekly stipend, included the keeping of the cottage and its contents in perfect order.

Thus, having succeeded in the quest, we departed from Stratford-on-Avon, to which we may return some day, perhaps when it has lost its celebrity, not because it is the birthplace of Shakespeare, but when he shall no longer be regarded as the Author of Shakespeare's Plays.

THE END

Colston & Coy. Limited, Printers, Edinburgh

www.ingramcontent.com/pod-product-compliance
Lightning Source LLC
Chambersburg PA
CBHW030435190426
43202CB00036B/965